Patrick Donan, Cy Warman

Utah

A Peep into a Mountain Walled Treasury of the Gods

Patrick Donan, Cy Warman

Utah

A Peep into a Mountain Walled Treasury of the Gods

ISBN/EAN: 9783337049898

Printed in Europe, USA, Canada, Australia, Japan

Cover: Foto ©Andreas Hilbeck / pixelio.de

More available books at **www.hansebooks.com**

I would know my native land

There are those who praise the poet who can soar in starry spheres,
 And can mould his mystic phrases from the wrecks of other years;
I would have my inspiration fresh from nature's open hand -
 I would sing a simple sonnet that a child can understand.

There are those who seek in other climes the joys they might have known
 Mid the mountains and the meadows of the land they call their own.
I would seek the shady canyons where at night the gentle dew
 Comes to kiss the rose and heliotrope when stars are all in view.

I would walk the verdant valley where the salt waves wash the feet
 Of the Wasatch. Gazing upward where the sky and mountains meet,
Filled with awe and admiration I would kneel upon the strand,
 And thank heaven for this picture even I can understand.

I would stand amid these mountains with their hueless caps of snow,
 Looking down the distant valley stretching far away below;
And with reverential rapture thank my Maker for this grand,
 Peerless, priceless panorama that a child can understand.

RHYMES BY CY WARMAN

UTAH LAKE

An' blest are we who walk upon the shore
When daylight dies;
Here, where's some hint of rapture evermore
Beyond the skies.

Sangre de Cristo, let me trace
The beauties of thy furrowed face;
  While poncha-perfumed summer breeze
  Makes music in thine arboles.

I.

INTRODUCTORY.

THE FOLLY OF AMERICANS WHO TRAVEL ABROAD BEFORE THEY HAVE SEEN THEIR OWN COUNTRY.

EASTERN newspaper statisticians are proverbially masters of the art of inaccuracy, and their so-called statistics are usually to be taken, like dreams or women's whims, by contraries. But they are probably not far wrong in their every-season estimate that a hundred thousand Americans annually make the tour of Europe at an average expense of at least a thousand dollars each. That is a total of a hundred million dollars a year expended by new-world people in familiarizing themselves with old-world scenes, while, as a general thing, they are wholly unacquainted with the infinitely grander scenes on their own side of the Atlantic ferry. In a single day of the recent season eight huge ocean steamers left New York, bearing nearly three thousand first-cabin passengers for a European summer tour. Every steamship that sails during the fashionable outing months goes crowded with these too often ignorant and snobocratic American voyagers to foreign lands for recreation and pleasure, that could be far more easily and cheaply found at home. How many of them have ever seen the glories and grandeurs, the beauties and sublimities of their own matchless land? How many of them know, how many of them have ever dreamt, that their own — our own — is incomparably the grandest continent on all the globe?

There is urgent need of a constitutional amendment prohibiting any untutored American citizen or citizeness, redolent of pork corners, wheat gouges, stock swindles, and "just-struck-rich-dirt"-inesses, from going abroad to paralyze the cab-drivers and coffee-house waiters of effete monarchies with gilded republican airs until he or she has seen and learned something of America. It should require, as an inexorable condition-precedent for permission to squander American gold and silver in London haberdashers' establishments and Parisian milliners' shops, and to go into cheap raptures — after careful consultation of the guide-books — over Italian skies and mole-hills, duck-ponds and dilapidated macaroni hasheries, a certificate from the president and general manager of some such great system of American railway as the Rio Grande Western, Denver & Rio Grande, and Colorado Midland, that the would-be foreign voyager had visited all the wondrous and glorious scenes along their lines. It would be an admirable educational measure. It would give tens of thousands of semi-bogus Americans — native-born aliens — some idea of the grandeur of their own country, and prevent them from making the lavish displays of ignorance and stupidity with which they now amuse or disgust the first intelligent man or woman they meet after setting foot on European soil.

It was Byron who, meeting one of these typical American tourists in Florence, eagerly exclaimed : " Tell me of Niagara Falls ! Describe your great cataract to me ! " When the American shamefacedly confessed he had never seen the cataractic wonder of the world, the poet abruptly turned on his heel and left him, denouncing as " a d———d fool " any man who, without having seen Niagara, would come from America to Europe to sham ecstacy over pigmy mountains and lakes and rivers. And the lame author of " Childe Harold " was not too severe.

The more one sees of our majestic half-world — our continental American republic — the less patience he must have with those absurd creatures who, every year, flock by tens of thousands to other lands, while they have seen nothing and know nothing of their own. Earth has no other land like ours. Among all the nationalities and realms of the globe, " Columbia, the Gem of the Ocean," is peerless, unrivaled and unrivalable, unapproached and unapproachable. The grandest empires of the old world, of ancient or of modern times, sink to petty provinces beside its vast dimensions. The whole possessions of Rome, when her golden eagles spread their wings victorious from the burning sands of Africa to the mist-clad hills of Caledonia, fell short of the immensity of our new-world domain. Russia, vastest of modern sovereignties, could be lost in our half-hemisphere beyond the power of all the buzzards in Christendom to find her. France, land of Napoleon, at the tread of whose legions but three quarters of a century ago all Europe trembled as if taken with a Wabash-valley ague, would scarcely overlap the single Territory of Utah ; while Great

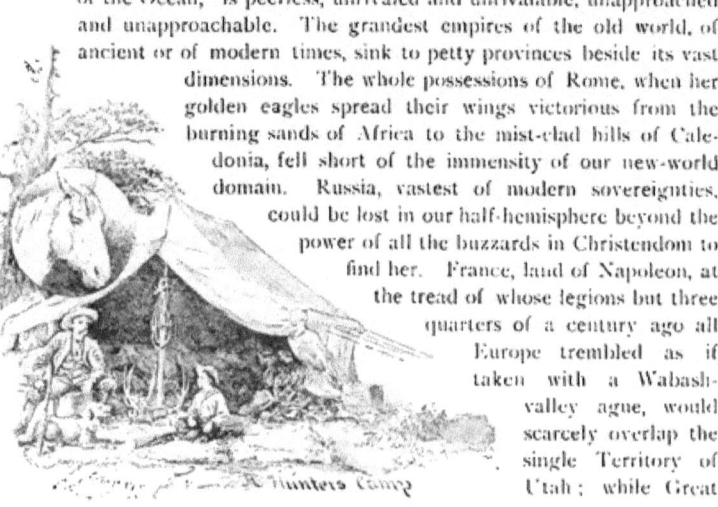

Canyon of the Grand

THE ACROPOLIS OF THE DESERT.

Britain, whose morning drum-beat sounds around the globe, would hardly make a fly-speck on the face of Texas or California.

Do other lands boast of their great rivers? We could take up all their Niles and Thameses, their yellow Tibers, castled Rhines and beautiful blue Danubes by their little ends, and empty them into our majestic Mississippis and Missouris, Columbias and Rio Grandes, Amazons, Saskatchewans and De La Platas without making rise enough to lift an Indiana flat-boat off a sandbar. Do they brag of their seas and lakes? We could spill all their puny Caspians and Azovs, Nyanzas and Maggiores, into our mighty Superiors, Michigans, Hurons, Eries and Ontarios, and scarce produce a ripple on their pebbled brims to wash away the eighteen-inch "foot-print on the sands of time" left by the fairy-like slipper of a St. Louis or Chicago girl; while in any ring, Marquis of Queensbury rules, our Wasatch-walled Great Salt Lake could strip the championship belt for mystery and majesty from their long-famed, Sodom-engulfing, weird Dead Sea. Do they prate of their romantic scenery? We have a thousand jewel-like lakes that would make all their vaunted Comos, Genevas and Killarneys hide their faces in a veil of friendly fog. The rolling thunder of our Niagara drowns out the feeble murmur of all their cataracts; while the awful crags and canyons of our Yellowstone and Yosemite, Gunnison, Arkansas and Colorado; the prismatic glitter and dash of our Minnehahas, Shoshones and Ocklawahas; and the lonely grandeur of our horizon-fenced prairies, boundless oceans of billowy verdure, dwarf to insipidity the most famous scenes of Switzerland and Italy, eclipse the wonders and glories of the Arabian Nights, and defy all the skill of poet's pen and artist's pencil to depict the veriest atom of their sublimity and their loveliness. Do they prattle about their .Etnas and Vesuviuses? With our noses turning somersets of ineffable contempt clear over our heads, we thunder forth our Cotopaxis, Popocatapetls, Chimborazos and a score of other jawbreakers whose very names alone are too huge for common tongues. (It is true that some of these specimens of national prodigiousness do not just exactly belong to us yet ; but they belong to our next-door neighbors, who are not as strong as we are, and to the gloriously expansive spirit of Yankee progress, where or what is the difference?) Do other lands and nations talk of their mines of jewels and gold? We answer with the exhaustless bonanzas of California, Colorado, Montana, Idaho and Utah, where mountains of gold and silver ore challenge the skies, and where the ceaseless thunder of the world's greatest bullion-mills resounds in the yet warm lair of the Rocky Mountain grizzly bear. Do they rave of the harvest fields of Germany and Britain, and the vine-clad hills of France? We show them half a hemisphere, with soils and climates as varied as the tastes of men, and with capacities for production as boundless as the needs of men ; yielding everything, cereal, vegetable, animal, textile and mineral, agricultural, horticultural, geological, zoölogical, pomological, piscatorial, and ornithological, ovine, bovine, capricornine and equine, that all the wants of all the races, tribes, kindreds and tongues of earth can ever require. The sun in heaven, in all his grand rounds since "the evening and the morning were the first day," never looked down on a more magnificent domain — a fresh and glorious half-world, grand in all its proportions, and endlessly diversified, rich and gorgeous in all its adornments, resting like a vast emerald breastpin upon the bosom of four great oceans. It is the broadest land ever given to any people, the grandest and most beautiful, the most varied in its productions, and the most unlimited in its capabilities, and its future. Other lands surpass it only in age and ruins. Time, if we wait long enough, will remedy the deficiency in age ; and we are already able to show some rather picturesque, though by no means majestic, ruins after every presidential election.

THE GARB OF THE HILLS.

Go visit the hills in the springtime,
　　When the little buds burst on the trees,
And the perfume of piñon and wild flowers
　　Is borne on the breath of the breeze.
When the rivulets leap from the snowlands,
　　As down toward the valley they sing,
To gladden the rose-laden low-lands—
　　Go visit the hills in the spring!

And then, when the summer is over,
　　And the dead leaves are strewn o'er the land,
When the blossoms have dropped from the clover,
　　A garment more gorgeous and grand
Is worn by the hills. True, the verdure,
　　The green and the freshness of spring
Have changed—the flowers have faded—
　　The song-birds are ceasing to sing.

But look! in the morn, when the sunlight
　　First flashes its rays o'er the range,
Ever changing anon till the wan light
　　Of evening is on—note each change—
Blends the fire and flame of the oak tree
　　With the gold of the aspen so tall;
All the radiant rays of the rainbow
　　Are worn by the hills in the fall.

II.

STILL INTRODUCTORY.

A Gentle Rap at the Too-Prevalent American Ignorance of America.

OF ALL this magnificent, more than imperial domain, one of the fairest garden spots is Utah. Yes, gentle or ungentle reader, as the case may be, you deciphered it aright — the word is Utah. You do not know where it is? That is not surprising. There is nothing of which the average intelligent American knows less than he does of the geography of his own country. Utah? You never heard of it except as a wild, far-away spot in a dismal wilderness, where every shrub has a cactus thorn and conceals a stinging reptile, and where the very waters heave up brimstone, pitch and ashes — a sort of cross between Hades and the Great Sahara, the fitting home of a horde of semi-savage fanatics known as Mormons? Very likely. Your ignorance is not exceptional. Even educated Americans are phenomenal in the profundity and variety of what they do not know in regard to every region and characteristic of their native land beyond the range of their own chimneys' smoke. They laugh at foreigners for mixing up New York and San Francisco, and expecting to find buffaloes and warwhooping Indians in the suburbs of Cincinnati and Chicago; while, in nine hundred and ninety-nine cases out of every possible thousand, they show little greater knowledge than the more excusable blunderers they deride.

At a dinner given in New Orleans, a few years ago, to a Dakota man, a lady prominent in Crescent City society said to the guest of the occasion: "I understand, sir, you live in Dakota. You probably know a friend of mine, Mr. William Jones, out there?" The Dakotan turned to see if she was not simply guying him; but, perceiving that she was in earnest, replied: "In what part of Dakota, madam, does your acquaintance live?" "I think," she answered, "in a little place called Yankton. Isn't there a town of that name out there?" "Yes, madam," was the grave rejoinder; "but are you

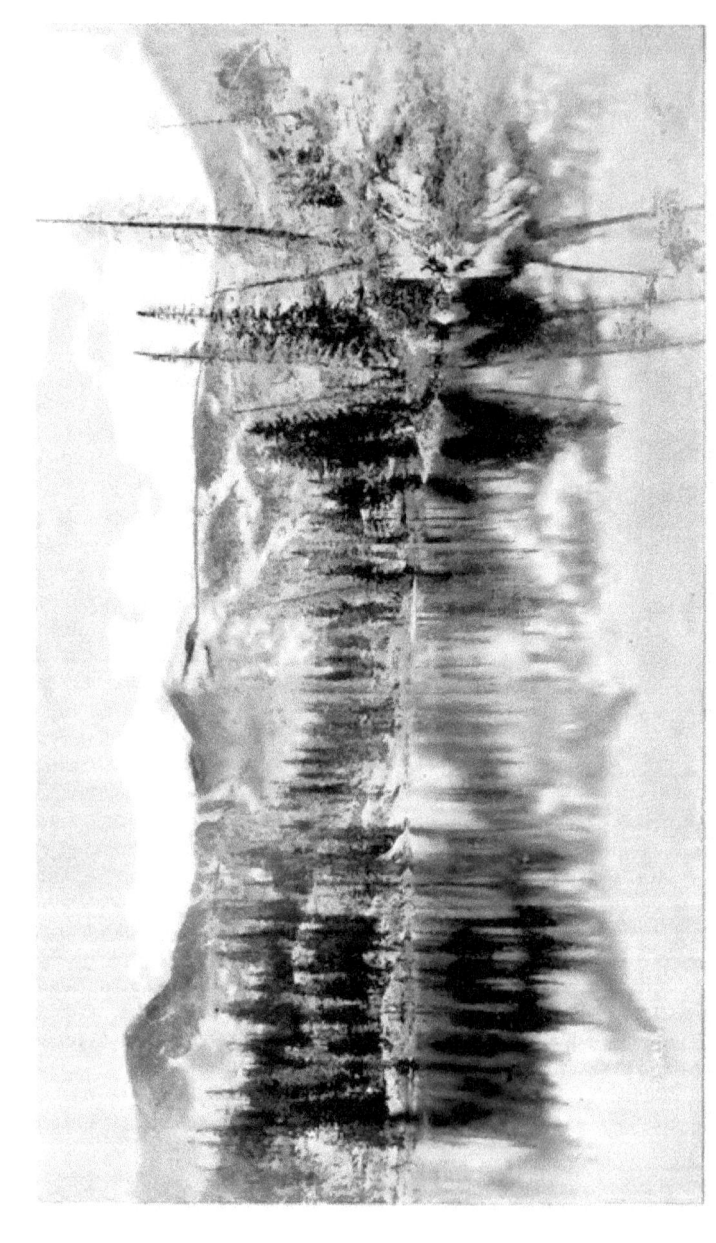

aware that, from my home on Devil's Lake, Dakota, to Yankton, where you think your friend, Mr. Jones, resides, by the shortest travelable route, is about eight hundred miles, or just one hundred and fifteen miles less than from New Orleans to Chicago?" The statement, at that time, was absolutely true, but the man who made it was promptly set down by every guest at the table, as the worst specimen of wild-western Munchausenism that had ever appeared in New Orleans.

So, esteemed madam, miss or sir, if ignorance, like misery, loved company, you would have abundance of it, even among our most cultivated people. Your lack of knowledge as to Utah is not unparalleled, but it will hereafter be unpardonable, or this brief dissertation will have failed in its mission. A few moments of your valuable time and attention and you will know considerably more than you do, and still be just as handsome as you are.

A theme so vast and varied, so rich and beautiful, appropriately begins a new chapter.

III.

UTAH.

A Brief General Outline, Geographical, Scenic and Resourceful, of a Wonderful Region.

UTAH extends from 37° to 42° North latitude, and from 32° to 37° West longitude, and is an almost exact square, three hundred miles each way. It has an area of 87,750 square miles, or 52,601,600 acres ; of which 2,780 square miles, or 1,776,200 acres, are water. It is 11,420 square miles, or 7,308,800 acres, larger than Maine, New Hampshire, Vermont, Massachusetts, Rhode Island, Connecticut, New Jersey and Delaware, all combined ; and there is no region of equal area on the globe, that overflows with more abounding and diversified riches of resource and possibility.

Utah was first settled by a detachment of Mormons, under the leadership of Brigham Young, in July, 1847 ; and there is no stronger argument in favor of the Mormon claim to divine revelations and inspirations, than the fact that they should have been led through nearly three thousand miles of unexplored wilderness, infested at every step by hostile savages, to such a "Land of Promise," where every promise finds so glorious fulfillment. Guided by the Jehovah-swayed "pillar of cloud by day, and pillar of fire by night," Israel of old wandered forty years in search of a "promised land" that would hardly make a cow-lot in Utah.

Lift all New England and New York bodily a mile above the level of the sea. Add five thousand feet to the height of Mount Washington, and seven thousand to that of Mount Mitchell. Throw in dozens of other peaks fully as high, all punching holes in the sky with their snowy crowns. Pile up, everywhere, hundreds on hundreds of mountains from ten to fourteen thousand feet high. Exaggerate fifty-fold all the wild notches and gorges and glens of eastern America, and multiply them by scores. Send cataracts and cascades leaping and foaming down a thousand dizzy precipice channels. Toss in, promiscuously, parks larger than whole States in the tame, smallnotioned east; and gardens of giant statuary — statues of gods and genii and gnomes, Titans, Centaurs, and un-named monsters, thousands of feet high — hewn by ages on ages of winds and waves and whirling waters Cap all the mountain-tops with everlasting ice and snow, and clothe their shaggy sides with waving forests of valuable timber. Fill all the valleys to the mountains' feet with orchards and gardens, vineyards and grain-fields, bending beneath the burdens of their own magnificent fruitage; and dot the horizon-bounded pasture-lands with flocks and herds, waist-deep in the very wantonness of plenty. Underlay the whole vast area with gold and silver, zinc, copper, lead and iron ores; marble of a hundred hues; anthracite, bituminous and cannel coal; salt, sulphur, soda, lime and gypsum; and nearly every other metal and mineral in human use. Through countless wondrous canyons, pour mighty rivers with water-power enough to run all the world's machinery. Smite the rock-ribbed laboratories of Omnipotence, and let unnumbered healing floods gush forth, rich in miracle-working virtues for the alleviation of many of the sorest "ills that flesh is heir to." As the dazzling bosom-jewel of the whole transcendent scene, spread out the twenty-five hundred square miles of that majestic and mysterious lake, whose waters hold in solution wealth enough to pay all the national debts of the world, and leave a fortune for every man, woman and child from Cape Cod to Yuba Dam. And over all throw the glory of a climate unsurpassed under heaven since sin and death climbed into Eden, and the translucent splendor of skies more radiantly sapphirean than ever bent their crystal arches above the far-famed, beggar-hemmed and flea-girt Bay of Naples, or the Lake of Como, on whose enchanted shores lay the bogus ranch of that glib-tongued bunco-steerer, Claude Melnotte — And — you have a poor, faint, puny approximation to an idea of Utah!

It is a land where mountains of gold and silver ore, that runs from fifty to five thousand dollars to the ton, wall in valleys that yield from sixty to eighty bushels of wheat, from seventy-five to a hundred bushels of oats, and from five hundred to nine hundred bushels of potatoes, to the acre. It is a land where every man makes his own rain, and the crops never fail; where the rewards of industry are as sure as the decrees of God; where wonder treads on beauty's heels, and riches rush to meet the earnest seeker. Its resources are as boundless as its limits, and as varied as the ever-changing hues that bathe its sunsets in prismatic splendors. Here is Ute-opia indeed!

What is there that the imagination of man can conceive, or his eye, heart, soul, stomach or pocket can desire, that Utah does not yield, or cannot offer? Is it scenery or climate? Is it health or wealth, fertile farms, bonanza mines, or lovely homes? Is it opportunities for profitable investments, or openings for all varieties of labor and of enterprise?

Let a fresh chapter begin the brief reply.

The Canyon of the Grand.

I'm going to paint a picture with a pencil of my own.
   I shall have no hand to help me, I shall paint it all alone;
Oft I fancy it before me as my hopeful heart grows faint!
   As I contemplate the grandeur of the picture I would paint.

When I rhyme about the river, the laughing limpid stream,
   Whose ripples seem to shiver as they glide and glow and gleam,
Of the waves that beat the boulders that are strewn upon the strand,
   You will recognize the river in the Canyon of the Grand.

When I write about the mountains with their heads so high and hoar,
   Of the cliffs and craggy canyons where the waters rush and roar,
When I speak about the walls that rise so high on either hand,
   You will recognize the rockwork in the Canyon of the Grand.

God was good to make the mountains, the valleys and the hills,
   Put the rose upon the cactus the ripple on the rills;
But if I had all the words of all the worlds at my command,
   I couldn't paint a picture of the Canyon of the Grand.

IV.

CLIMATE AND HEALTH.

UTAH AS ONE OF THE WORLD'S GRANDEST SANITARIUMS—
SOME NOVEL AND STRIKING FACTS.

"We believe it is a duty to live past seventy."—

grandeur and loveliness of Utah scenery have already been touched upon, and are so interwoven with its mines and meadows, fields, forests, lakes, valleys, and every other feature and interest, that they will find frequent mention hereafter. It is a tourist's paradise, a true holy land of sight-seers and lovers of nature in her sublimest and most entrancing moods, a realm of beauty and a joy forever to the artist soul. What of its climate and healthfulness?

Climate is not regulated by latitude. Ocean currents and altitude are potent factors in it. The snows of untold ages lie unmelted on the lofty peaks of the Cordilleras in Mexico, the Andes in South America, and the Himalayas in Hindostan. Alaska, in the latitude of Greenland, has a climate little more rigorous than that of Ohio. Washington and Oregon, in the latitude of hard-frozen Maine and blizzardy Dakota, where it is mid-winter seven months of the year, and very late in the fall the other five, bask in the sunny mildness of Virginia and Carolina ; and California, on the same parallels with Nebraska, Kansas and Oklahoma, raises oranges, bananas, pine-apples, figs, lemons and pomegranates. Utah, in the latitude of Missouri, where the mercury often runs the whole length of the thermometer in twenty-four hours, enjoys a climate as balmy and as equable as the airs that breathe over Araby the Blest. For fourteen years the mean temperature in Salt Lake City was about fifty-two degrees, the average maximum being ninety-seven degrees, the average minimum minus one, and the mean daily range of the mercury but twenty degrees. Cotton grows luxuriantly in the southern part of the territory, and all the semi-tropical fruits flourish everywhere within its borders; and yet there is not a day in the year when one cannot, if he will, wallow in a snowdrift fifty feet deep, or seat himself on an iceberg a hundred yards square, by climbing a few miles up a mountain-side. During the month of August, 1891, the whole eastern and southern portion of the United States, and even the vauntedly paradisiacal Northwest, sweltered and seethed with torrid heat. Apples baked on the trees around Chicago, that brazenly proclaims itself "the great lake-side summer resort of North America." People died of sunstrokes and calorical prostrations from Winnepisseogee to Corpus Christi — that is, from Maine to Texas. Even in the alleged "glorious summer climate" of Minnesota and Dakota, the thermometers boiled over with a hundred and ten to a hundred and fifteen degrees of hideous hotness in the shade. Milwaukee refrigerators turned to steam-boilers ; pop-corn popped instead of sprouting in the Iowa and Missouri hills, and a universal wail of sweaty anguish went up to skies of red-hot brass from the whole wretched land and people. And, in all the time, there was not a night that Salt Lake City people did not sleep under blankets, and not a day when they could not see the huge masses of snow on the Wasatch Mountains glistening white and cold in the August sunshine ; while, at the base of the mountains, which slope down almost into the eastern edge of the city, the whole earth was hidden in the foliage and fruit and flowers of orchards and vineyards and gardens. Low latitude gives heat, and high altitude gives cold ; so every fellow can mix his own climate and weather to suit himself. Here, as nearly as anywhere else in the temperate zone, might be realized that boyish ideal of a home : A tall, glacier-crested mountain in a tropical region. At its base, plantations of sugar, coffee, rice, indigo, and spices ; orange, palm and mango groves ; and forests of mahogany, ebony and rosewood, with myriads of gorgeous-plumaged parrots, toucans and macaws flitting like winged bits of rainbows among their leafy boughs. Midway up the sloping side, at an elevation of eight or ten thousand feet, fields of corn, wheat, oats and barley; orchards of apples, pears, plums and cherries ;

Rugged Crags

meadows of honey-scented clover, the hum of bees, the lowing of cattle, bubbling springs, coveys of quails, and cooing doves. And at the summit a mighty storehouse of everlasting snow and ice to cool the juleps and tequilla. So that, with a tiny inclined railroad ten or fifteen miles long, one could slide through all climates and seasons, from perpetual summer to eternal winter and back again, in half an hour, in any day of all the year. In Utah the torrid feature alone would be lacking in this grand climatic climacteric — this having, like death, "all seasons for one's own."

Weather-bureau statistics show that the sun shines all day over three hundred days in every year in Utah, and there are few of the remaining days in which it does not brighten part of the hours. There are but two places in the United States, El Paso and Santa Fé, where observation shows less humidity in the atmosphere than at Salt Lake City. The air is so dry and pure, that the carcasses of dead animals do not putrefy; they simply dry up without offensive odor. So crystalline is the clearness of the wonderful atmosphere, that it is impossible for eyes accustomed to less favored regions to form any correct estimate of distances out here. No stranger to this ethereal purity can realize that it is more than a mile or two from the Temple Square in Salt Lake City to the summits of the Wasatch Mountains, and yet they are twenty long miles away. No eye, inured to the atmospheric murkiness of New York or Chicago, can make the strip of blue-green water between Lake Park bathing-beach and Antelope Island in Great Salt Lake seem wider than the Upper Hudson or Ohio River ; though it would take a nine-mile pull to cross it at its narrowest place. With its marvelous commingling of salt-sea air and mountain ozone, with its highness and dryness, with an atmosphere as soft and pure as that which fanned the cheek of sinlessness in primeval paradise, Utah is one of the world's great natural sanitariums. Catarrh, hayfever and asthma vanish at once beneath its balmy influence. Even tubercular consumption, in all its earlier stages, finds sure relief and cure. From the strange, Deity-wrought alchemies of the mountain sides all over the territory burst forth magical fountains of healing for invalids of almost every class. Nearly every variety of medicinal waters known to humanity is found somewhere in this pharmacopeian wonderland. Hot Springs, that possess all the virtues of those in Arkansas, pour hissing and steaming from the cliffs at Ogden, Salt Lake City, Castilla and a score of other places. Lithia Springs, as potent as those of Carlsbad or Homburg, and sulphur springs of every kind — white, red, black, blue and yellow, hot and cold — as well as soda, magnesia, alum,

Peaceful Plains.

and all the countless species of chalybeate waters. Great Salt Lake itself is a twenty-five-hundred-square-miles Bethesda Pool, where no angel's wing is needed to stir the healing virtues.

The sick and enfeebled of every region may here find some specific, compounded by the Great Physician's own all-wise hand, for their relief or cure. Hundreds, who first came to Utah, by prescription of their doctors, after having tried Arkansas, Colorado and New Mexico, scarcely hoping to find even temporary alleviation of the tortures of disease, now live in vigorous rejuvenation to sound the praises of the matchless Utah-land, which is destined to become one of the grandest health-resort regions of the world.

What is the one infallible test of the invigorating qualities of climate, atmosphere, and general conditions? Abundance of children and old people; and nowhere in America do both more plenteously abound than Utah. The old-time Mormon families of twenty, forty, sixty and, in some instances, over seventy children each, proclaim in trumpet tones the sturdy vigor and healthfulness of the race and region. Pleasant Grove, on the Rio Grande Western Railway, with a total population of twenty-three hundred, has eight hundred and sixty-two school children, and at least four hundred more under the school-going age; and Ephraim, with twenty-two hundred population, has over eight hundred school children, and three hundred and seventy-eight of younger growth. Salt Lake City is the only place of fifty thousand people in the United States, if not in the world, where baby-wagons are imported by the train-load, and where they have the right-of-way over even the electric cars.

And "extremes meet," for old people swarm everywhere. A quick-witted and nimble-footed old lady of eighty-three recently said to a newspaper correspondent: "We Mormons believe it is a duty to live past seventy;" and hosts of them discharge the "duty" without half trying. "Old Folks' Day" is a Utah Mormon institution, which might well be made national in its scope and observance. It was established by Bishop Hunter, of the Mormon Church, who died at the age of ninety years. It comes on the twenty-second of June, and is observed as a general holiday. An excursion is given to people of seventy years and upwards, winding up with a banquet, a dance, and a generous distribution of presents. In 1887, when Salt Lake City had but about thirty thousand population, she sent seven hundred and fifty of these ancient jollifiers, over the Rio Grande Western Railway, to Ogden. Of the number, a hundred and twelve ranged in age from eighty to ninety-seven. A seventy-year-old papa, trundling a baby-chariot, with the springy tread of a young game-rooster, is no uncommon sight on city street or country road.

Health, vigor, all glories of air, and climate, and human robustitude — Utah has them, and to spare.

V.

AGRICULTURAL AND PASTORAL.

The Marvelous Fertility of Utah Soil — Some Astonishing Illustrations.

NO PROPERLY constituted man could ever deliberately aspire to win fame as a successor of Ananias. And yet he, who sets out to tell the simplest, unsandpapered and unvarnished truths in regard to Utah, as a farmer-land, a home-land, foredooms himself to go galloping down the crookedest byways of public estimation, as a compeer of Sapphira's luckless spouse, and all the other puissant liars of ancient and modern days. But Utah truth is mighty, and must be told — even though he who tells it finds himself nailed by the ears to the pillory-posts of popular misjudgment, as a marvel of monumental mendacity.

One may have seen the valley of the Nile, for ages "the granary of the world." He may have roamed amid the rich plantations of the Caribbean shores, where the wondrous soil yields almost spontaneously every grain, grass, vegetable, fruit and fabric necessary for human sustenance and luxury. He may have roamed delighted over the sea islands of Georgia and Carolina, and the romance-haunted Teche region of Louisiana, "the land of Evangeline," where nature riots in wild luxuriance of production. He may have traversed the fertile Scioto Valley, the paradise of Ohio; and the far-famed Red River Valley of Dakota, with its mighty wheat-fields stretching away till, all around, the blue sky meets the heads of golden grain. He may have grown familiar with all the so-called garden-spots of earth:

but there are still amazements for him — in Utah. On all the beauteous, pendent globe, no fairer, richer realm unfolds itself to tempt the angels down. No mightier treasure-houses of royal ore rear their proud heads heavenward in any land or zone. No more overflowingly bounteous, golden grainfields or heavier-laden vines and fruit-trees ever gladdened the heart and pocket of sun-browned husbandman with hundred-fold harvests. No greener pastures ever feasted the frolicsome mule-colt, or fatted the festive gentleman-calf.

Here, Isaiah's millennial rhapsody of prediction finds literal fulfillment. The wilderness and the solitary place have been made glad, and the desert does rejoice and blossom as a rose. Where no water is, Utah soil is the picture of desolation. Nothing grows but cactus, grease weed, prairie dogs and Jack-rabbits. Turn on the water and a garden blooms. You touch the water button, and God and nature do the rest — and do it gloriously. All farming is by irrigation, and where every farmer makes his own season and controls his own rain, crop failures are unknown. There has never been one in Utah. No rain on the new mown hay, no drouth when the grain heads are filling. Water in abundance just when and where it is needed, and never and nowhere else. The soil is inexhaustible. No artificial fertilization has ever been used. Manure heaps are burned. Fields in the Salt Lake valley that have been cropped incessantly for forty years yield annually from fifty to seventy-five bushels of wheat, from six to ten tons of Lucerne clover and from five hundred to nine hundred bushels of potatoes to the acre, and everything else in proportion.

The official figures of the National Department of Agriculture show that the average wheat crop of the country is about twelve bushels to the acre, and that in the much-vaunted grain belt of Dakota it is scarcely thirteen bushels to the acre. In Utah sixty to seventy bushels to the acre is an ordinary yield. In 1889, the "American Agriculturist" prize for the largest yield of wheat to the acre in the United States was awarded to William Gibby, whose farm is a short distance south of Salt Lake City. His crop, raised on measured ground and every detail attested by reliable witnesses, was eighty-four bushels and ten pounds to the acre. John H. White, four miles north of Salt Lake City, in 1890, raised on twenty acres of land nineteen hundred and twenty bushels of oats, or ninety-six bushels to the acre. On the same land, the year before, he raised one hundred and four bushels to the acre. W. D. Major, near Bountiful, a little place that is certainly well named, north of Salt Lake City, in 1890, raised ninety bushels of barley to the acre. Utah does not claim to be a corn country, because many other crops are so much more profitable, but W. D. Major has recently raised fifty bushels of white flint corn to the acre; and Bailey & Son, sixty bushels of yellow corn to the acre. In 1890, Thomas Farrar, near Green River Station on the Rio Grande Western Railway, raised a hundred and twelve bushels

The Golden Tower, Kelso.

to the acre. Richard Carlisle, of Mill Creek, six miles south of Salt Lake City, in 1890, with irrigation from an artesian well, raised nine hundred and forty-seven bushels of potatoes to the acre, and sold them at eighty cents a bushel, realizing in cash $767.60 an acre for one year's crop. Mr. Culmer, at Pleasant Grove, thirty miles south of Salt Lake City, cleared $1,200 an acre on strawberries in a single season. John H. White, whose hundred-and-four-bushels-to-the-acre oats crop has already been mentioned, in 1890 cut three crops of alfalfa or lucerne clover from his meadow, amounting to seven tons to the acre. He sold it in the Salt Lake market at fourteen dollars a ton, making ninety-eight dollars an acre in cash for one season's hay crop. Four crops of alfalfa are frequently cut in a season, and from seven to ten tons is a common yield.

But why multiply such instances? Every one of those given is officially attested by the Salt Lake City Chamber of Commerce, and volumes might be filled with similar illustrations of the fiction-surpassing fertility of this wonderland of husbandry. Call the roll of products and there is none that can be raised in the temperate zone which does not reach perfection here. Earth is absolutely wanton in fecundity. Rye yields an average of from sixty to seventy bushels to the acre; turnips, from four hundred to six hundred bushels; carrots, from seven hundred to a thousand bushels; apricots, three hundred and fifty to five hundred bushels; peaches, from five hundred to seven hundred bushels; apples, four hundred and fifty to six hundred bushels; pears, five hundred bushels; plums, from three hundred to four hundred bushels; blackberries, raspberries, currants and gooseberries, from three hundred to three hundred and fifty bushels to the acre, and everything else in like profusion. Cherries grow wild in great abundance. Hops are indigenous to the soil. Nectarines flourish everywhere, and figs are raised in the southern valleys. Cotton grows luxuriantly in the lower counties, and a cotton mill established by the Mormons at Washington has long been in successful operation. It uses about 75,000 pounds of cotton yearly and manufactures good domestics.

In the Chamber of Commerce at Salt Lake City is a wonderful collection of cabinets and cases, that were sent east in 1887 in "The Utah Exposition Car," which traveled twelve thousand miles, and was visited by over two hundred thousand people. In the collection there are jars of plums fully as large as ordinary eastern pears; gooseberries as large as full-sized plums; and strawberries as big as large tomatoes, many of them being from ten to twelve inches in circumference, and thirteen of them filling a quart jar. Sugar beets

weighing thirty-five pounds each, mangel wurzels weighing forty-eight pounds and Irish potatoes weighing from eight to eight and a half pounds apiece, are included in the collection. Potatoes, twelve or fifteen of which make a bushel, are common in the markets. Melons of all kinds grow to great size, and are deliciously flavored. The very streets are shaded with fruit trees, and the humblest adobe cottage is hidden in its wealth of apple, pear and plum, apricot, peach and nectarine trees, bending beneath their luscious freightage. Salt Lake is always compared to the Dead Sea, but no "Dead Sea apples," fair to the eye, but ashes to the lips, grow upon its blessed shores

Stock-raising in Utah involves but little care or labor. Pasture is found the year round, and all domestic animals thrive on the native grasses of the mesas and valleys. There are now in the territory about five hundred thousand cattle, two hundred and fifty thousand horses and mules, a hundred thousand hogs, and two and a half million sheep, worth, all told, something near thirty million dollars.

Utah produced in 1890 about twelve million pounds of wool, of which one million pounds was manufactured in home mills and factories, and the rest exported. In the Salt Lake Chamber of Commerce are forty samples of merino wool furnished by Charles Crane, of Kanosh, Kanab County, president of the Utah Wool Growers' Association. The forty fleeces from which the samples were taken weighed from forty-one to sixty-seven pounds each. Think of it! Sixty-seven pounds of merino wool clipped from a single sheep — more than a whole sheep, bones, mutton, tallow, hide and all, often weighs in the hapless East.

With a soil of such matchless fertility; with a climate unsurpassed and unsurpassable; with ten thousand square miles of timber lands; with boundless ranges for flocks and herds; with exhaustless mines in a hundred rugged mountain-sides; and with millions of acres yet subject to Government entry, what does Utah lack to render it the ideal land of the farmer and home-seeker? It is, in the language of Holy Writ, "A land of brooks of water; of fountains and depths, that spring out of valleys and hills; a land of wheat and barley; a land wherein thou shalt eat bread without scarceness; thou shalt not lack anything in it."

Utah is an 87,750-square-mile cornucopia.

VI

UTAH MINES.

The Amazing Mineral Wealth and Possibilities of the Territory — A True Bonanza Land.

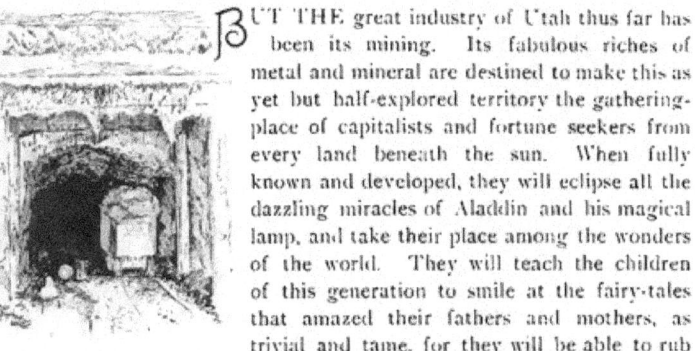

BUT THE great industry of Utah thus far has been its mining. Its fabulous riches of metal and mineral are destined to make this as yet but half-explored territory the gathering-place of capitalists and fortune seekers from every land beneath the sun. When fully known and developed, they will eclipse all the dazzling miracles of Aladdin and his magical lamp, and take their place among the wonders of the world. They will teach the children of this generation to smile at the fairy-tales that amazed their fathers and mothers, as trivial and tame, for they will be able to rub daily against the jewel-clad creatures of infinitely more marvelous stories in real life.

The greatest mines of earth are yet to be opened in the American Great West. Mountains of gold and silver ore, beside which all the famed riches of the Comstock Lode will some day sink to beggars' pence, yet rear their proud heads to heaven untouched by pick or spade or drill. The veritable treasure-houses of the gods yet await the enterprise and muscle of the sturdy prospectors and miners, who are destined, and that ere long, to fire the avarice and the envy of the world with their Midas-surpassing wealth of solid ducats. From Alaska to Nicaragua, the whole vast system of Rocky Mountains and Cordilleras is an almost unbroken ore and mineral bed. Not one ten-thousandth part of it has ever felt the tap of a prospector's hammer. The surface dirt of California, Colorado, Utah, Idaho, Montana, Arizona and New Mexico mines is hardly broken; the glittering hoards are scarcely touched. The great bonanza fortunes are yet to be made.

Although Utah mining is in the ruffled-cap and nursing-bottle stage of its existence, in its earliest infancy the territory has already produced a grand aggregate of about $175,000,000 in gold, silver, copper and lead; or more than the whole assessed valuation of such states as Wyoming and North Dakota. According to the official report of the United States Treasury Department for 1890, Utah now stands third among all the forty-nine states and territories of the Union, as a producer of the precious metals. With its magnificent yield for the year of $14,346,783 in

gold, silver, copper and lead. it leads California, with a total of $13,370,406; and Nevada, with but $8,543,800. Its yearly product is more than four times as great as that of all the mines of the famous Black Hills of Dakota; and it is outranked only by Montana with a total of $40,695,723; and Colorado, with $34,028,701. Its yield of four metals in 1890 amounted to nearly one-third of the entire assessed value of all real estate and personal property within its borders in 1888. There are mines in every county of the territory. Every mountain range and spur is ribbed with ore and mineral.

The accidental turning of a loose stone among the bushes in Ontario Gulch, in Summit county, led to the discovery of one of the world's greatest bonanzas. The prospect-hole was sold to a firm of which the late Senator Hearst, of California, was a member, for $30,000; and, as the Ontario mine, has since produced over $25,000,000 in silver, and paid $12,200,000 in dividends. Its mill and mining plant cost $2,700,000, and its annual pay-roll amounts to nearly $600,000. During 1890 it paid out in wages and salaries, for supplies, and in dividends, $2,017,055. The Daly mine, adjoining the Ontario, in 1890 produced $834,818, and paid $450,000 in dividends, making an aggregate of $1,762,500 in dividends since February, 1886. There are a hundred smaller mines in the same district, all more or less developed. The Crescent has yielded $1,500,000. The Woodside produced $444,000 in 1889. The Samson turned out about $250,000 worth of ore in 1890; and scores of others only need the capital and energy to convert them into bonanzas great or small. Park City, the metropolis of the district, is a picturesque place of five thousand population, which has no debt, and at the end of 1890 had twelve thousand dollars in its treasury. Its main street is seven thousand five hundred feet, or about a mile and a half, above the level of the sea. Its water supply is piped from Highland Lake, a liquid jewel of the Wasatch mountains, ten acres in extent, forty feet deep, and two thousand feet above the city. The camp produced in 1890 a grand total of 153,031,650 pounds of ore, an increase of 6,120,740 pounds over 1889. Of this, 63,297,650 pounds were shipped by rail to distant smelters, and 89,734,000 pounds were reduced at the home mills. A single chimney of ore at the east foot of the Grampian mountain in Beaver county, yielded over $13,000,000 in four years, and made the Horn Silver mine famous throughout the world. There are innumerable mines in the same region that only need proper work to make them rich producers.

At Alta, on Little Cottonwood Canyon, in Salt Lake county, almost in sight of Salt Lake City, is the renowned Emma mine, which wrecked the

reputation of one who had held high positions in the military, political and diplomatic service of the United States. An amazingly rich body of ore had been struck. For a long time the mine shipped a hundred tons a day of ore that ran from two hundred to seven hundred ounces of silver to the ton. General Schenck was then minister to England. He and his associates capitalized the mine in London at $5,000,000. The new company took out $1,500,000 in a few months, and then came a collapse. The ore disappeared, vanished like a fog-bank. The mine ceased producing. It looked like a gigantic swindle. General Schenck was ruined. The United States Minister to the Court of St. James had to fly from England to escape prosecution. It was the sensation of the day. Recent investigations and discoveries seem to indicate that the apparent failure was due to mistakes in the working of the mine. Experts say the company ran off the main ore-body, and followed side-slips. After years of loss a number of new strikes have been made, and the mine is again producing ore that runs one hundred and ten ounces of silver to the ton.

The Flagstaff, a neighbor of the Emma, and also owned by an English company, formerly produced from a hundred to two hundred tons a day of low-grade ore. Then the ore body was lost for a long time, and has only recently been re-discovered after years of labor and expense. The mine is now turning out ore that runs from twenty to forty ounces of silver to the ton.

There were, at one time, nearly a hundred producing mines in this camp, but when the Emma and the Flagstaff ore-bodies seemed to fail, work on most of them was abandoned. The late discoveries in the two famous mines have started operations on some of these long-neglected properties, and rich strikes and a renewed boom are among every day's possibilities. Ten mines in the camp, during 1890, shipped nine hundred and eighty tons of ore that yielded from thirty-two to two hundred and seventy-five ounces of silver to the ton — averaging ninety and a half ounces.

On Big Cottonwood Canyon, in Salt Lake county, the Maxfield mine has recently become a dividend-payer. In the last six months of 1890 it produced eleven hundred tons of ore, running seventy ounces of silver to the ton. The Congo shows ore running forty per cent. lead, sixty-five ounces of silver, and from five to ten dollars in gold to the ton. The Reed & Benson mine has yielded $300,000; and there are a number of other mines that promise big bundles of bullion.

On Snake Creek, in Utah county, many rich prospects are being opened up, the great drawback being the lack of transportation. There is no railroad communication and the wagon road is steep and rugged. The Southern Tier mine has recently made some shipments of ore that runs a hundred and fifty ounces of silver to the ton; and the Newell, Steamboat and Levigneur claims are showing handsomely.

On American Fork, in Utah county, there are more than a hundred mines in all stages of development. The North Star, from mere exploring work, shipped in 1890 over thirty tons of ore, that ran in silver and lead about eighty dollars to the ton. The Flora shows surface ore running from eighty to a hundred and fifty ounces of silver to the ton, and from twenty-five to forty per cent. lead. The New Idea has a vein from eight to twenty-three feet thick. One shipment of its ore brought a hundred and seven dollars a ton. The Osborn No. 2 has turned out some ore that shows six hundred ounces of silver to the ton. The Milkmaid, Treasure-Consolidate, Kalamazoo, Pittsburg, Chicago and Superior and Silver-Bell are all in high grade ore, and there are dozens more only awaiting the touch of capital to put them among the great mines of the country.

In Wasatch county, valuable bodies of ore have been struck in the Glencoe, Wilson and Barrett, Lowell, McHenry, Hawkeye, Boulder, Free Silver, Wasatch and numerous others.

Twenty-seven miles southwest of Salt Lake City, on the Rio Grande Western Railway, in the wild and picturesque Bingham Canyon of the Oquirrh mountains, lies the first mining district organized in Utah, and the Old Jordan mine in this canyon was the first mine discovered in the territory. Its oxidized surface ores, at its intersection with the South Galena, yielded $2,000,000; and a million tons of quartz, that will run twenty dollars a ton, now lie in sight in the same locality, unmined, unhonored and unsung, because the gold and silver in it are so combined that no method has yet been devised to work it without losing one

or the other. Less than a mile north of the Jordan, on Carr Fork, is a mountain side containing hundreds of thousands of tons of the same queer quartz, bearing about ten dollars in gold and ten in silver to the ton. Fully 1,500,000 tons of quartz lying in plain view, every ton of it carrying twenty dollars in gold and silver, or a total of at least $30,000,000, only waiting for the right man, with the right process of extraction, to come along and make himself a rival of the Rothschilds.

But Bingham has millions of tons of reducible ores. The Oquirrh mountains, which rise to a height of 10,500 feet, are literally bulged out with ores that are easily and cheaply mined and milled. It has produced more silver-lead ores than any other camp in Utah, and is to-day the second camp in tonnage of ore shipped, being outranked only by Tintic. The mineral belt is about six miles long, and from a half-mile to two miles wide, and it is nearly all more or less developed.

The camp shipped 33,822 tons of ore in 1890, of which the South Galena shipped 9,620 tons ; the Brooklyn, 8,092 tons ; Yo Semite No. 2, 2,610 tons ; Old Telegraph, 2,500 ; Spanish, 2,100 ; Niagara, 1,500 ; Lead and Yo Semite No. 1, 1,396 ; Utah, 1,216 ; and the Winamuck, York, Highland, Dixon, Rough and Ready, Silver Hill, Markham, Silver Gauntlet, Buckeye, Silver Shield, Last Chance and Fireclay, from 102 to 715 tons, each. Forty other mines sent out a total of 1,423 tons.

The South Galena, Brooklyn, Niagara and Yo Semite have concentrating mills, and there are gold mills on the Stewart and Stewart No. 2 ; for, in addition to all the vast deposits of silver, there is an extensive field of free-milling gold ore, running from five to fifteen dollars to the ton.

Among a lifetime's experiences of travel, by every conveyance from an ocean steamer or a limited express train to a Carolina bull-chariot or an African dromedary, there is nothing more novel than a ride in the South Galena ore-cars from the mine to the Rio Grande Western Railway station. Thirty iron cars, each carrying two tons of ore, or concentrates, arranged in couples, with a combination engineer, conductor and brakeman, all in one, to every two cars. Four thousand feet descent in four miles, over a track so crooked that a black snake could hardly follow it without breaking his back. It is like riding a twisty streak of lightning down from the clouds to earth.

The Bingham mines give employment to from fifteen hundred to two thousand men, and the production is constantly and rapidly increasing. Many important discoveries of ore have been made during the year ending in August, 1891, and over two hundred new mines have been located in the district.

The Dry Canyon and Ophir mines, in Tooele county, during 1890 shipped between four and five thousand tons of ore that ran fifty-three per cent. lead, twenty-three ounces of silver and one dollar in gold to the ton.

"A land whose stones are iron, and out of whose hills thou mayest dig brass."—Deut. viii. 9.

The principal producers are the Honerine, Brooklyn, Elgin, Belfast, Trade Wind, Miner's Delight, Utah Gem, Monarch and Northern Delight, and the Buckhorn group.

Second in size and importance of all the mining camps in Utah, being surpassed only by the great bonanza district, which includes the Ontario and Daly mines, is Tintic in Juab county. It lies on the western slope of the Oquirrh mountains, about ninety miles a little west of south from Salt Lake City. It consists of a vast mineral belt or zone, or of three or four parallel ones. This great ore-channel is nine miles long from north to south, and one and a quarter miles wide from east to west. It runs solidly across to Rush Valley, and there sinks, and is held by experts to reappear at Bingham, thirty or forty miles away on an air line. The camp contains many wonderful mines, and new discoveries are being constantly made.

In 1890 the camp shipped 76,497 tons of ore that ran from fifty to a hundred and fifty dollars to the ton, and the shipments are steadily and rapidly increasing. The largest shippers for that year were the Bullion-Beck, 29,509 tons; Eureka Hill, 20,640; Mammoth, 9,590; Centennial-Eureka, 3,668; Treasure, 3,200; and Keystone, 1,700, while the Julian Lane, Eagle, Northern Spy, Tesora, Sioux, Sunbeam, Carissa and Governor shipped from 103 to 798 tons each. The total shipments for the first half of 1891 have run about 250 tons a day.

The Eureka Hill could have been bought a few years ago for a song. It is now shipping a hundred tons a day of ore that nets about fifty dollars a ton, or something like $150,000 a month. Its monthly pay-roll is about $25,000, and all other expenses say $10,000 a month; making a total monthly expenditure of $35,000, and leaving a trifle of $115,000 a month to be divided among its fortunate owners. It is capitalized in ten thousand shares, of which John Q. Packard, of Salt Lake City, and his brother's estate hold five thousand and one shares; Jacob Lawrence's estate, three thousand five hundred; and Justice Field, of the United States Supreme Court, and his son-in-law, George W. Whitney, fourteen hundred and ninety-nine. So from this one young mining camp in Utah a judge of the highest tribunal in the new world rakes in about $16,000 dollars a month, that is double his annual salary every thirty days.

The Centennial-Eureka has had a romantic experience. A few years ago its owners were almost driven to the wall to meet a note for $10,000, and offered half the mine as security for the money. They finally succeeded in borrowing it, but had to get an extension of time upon it. Three days afterward they shipped two car-loads of ore that netted them $27,000. It is now paying $60,000 a month in dividends.

The Mammoth, across the mountain, about a mile and a half southeast of the Eureka Hill, is said to have been traded some years ago for a few head of Texas steers. During 1890, it paid twelve regular dividends, and four extra ones, of $40,000 each, a total of $640,000 for the year. Two car-loads of its ore recently netted $78,000. One mass of fifty pounds, which was taken out and sent east, was nearly half pure gold. In this mine free gold is found in horn silver, a combination rarely, if ever, met with anywhere else.

By far the heaviest ore-shipper in the camp is the Bullion-Beck, which adjoins the Eureka Hill. Captain S. H. Smith, its superintendent, was for twenty years on the Comstock Lode, and had charge of the famous Belcher mine from its opening to its virtual collapse on its three-thousand-foot level, during which time $35,000,000 were taken out of it. The Bullion-Beck has a superb plant, including hoisting-works, air-compressor, dynamos, blacksmith and carpenter shops, assay office, and fire-apparatus ; the whole costing over three hundred thousand dollars. The ore runs from forty-five to a hundred ounces of silver, and from fifteen to twenty-five per cent. of lead, to the ton. The mine is capitalized at $1,000,000, and in 1890 paid $420,000 in dividends, or forty-two per cent, besides paying for all improvements and additions to machinery.

The Gemini group, just across the gulch north of the Bullion-Beck, includes the Keystone, Excelsior, Red Bird and a number of others. Captain John McCrystal, the superintendent and part-owner, is also superintendent of the Eureka Hill, and of the Eagle and Godiva groups. The Gemini has shipped during 1891, about fifty tons a day of ore that nets in the neighborhood of fifty dollars a ton.

The Eagle is a new mine, but five hundred and ninety tons of its ore, shipped between September 21, 1890, and August 1, 1891, netted $45,000, after paying in freights and for reduction about $17,000 ; giving an average yield of $110 to the ton.

The Godiva shows ore carrying twenty-five dollars a ton in gold. The Northern Spy produced $400,000 above its first level. The Plutus, Snowflake, Sioux, Iron Blossom, Turk, Hungarian, Daisy, Lucky Boy, Belcher group, Alamo, Golden Ray group and a legion of others are all working in ore that is rich enough to satisfy any reasonable would-be bonanza-king.

The Dragon mine, during 1890, shipped to the smelters near Salt Lake City 6,050 tons of iron ore for fluxing purposes. Nearly all the Tintic mines are worked by their owners or leasers, who, with few exceptions, started in poor men. The fame of its riches has begun to reach the outer world. New men are pouring in; new claims are being located in every direction; long-abandoned "prospects" are being re-opened and worked; a branch of the Rio Grande Western Railway is nearing the camp as rapidly as men and money can push it; and there is every indication of a great boom throughout the whole region. Its marvelous wealth, and the opportunities it offers for men of nerve and enterprise, cannot be over-estimated.

Jay Gould has never been charged with extravagance or over-enthusiasm in his estimates of anything belonging to somebody else. On the twenty-fourth of August, 1891, he and his party, including his two daughters and two of his sons, with a special train of four cars, ran into Eureka, the capital of the Tintic district, to the astonishment of the citizens. The whole party, including the Wall-street Wizard, made a tour of the Bullion-Beck mine and of the camp in general, and expressed in glowing terms their admiration of its rich possibilities. In an account of the visitation, The Salt Lake City *Tribune* of the next day said: "Mr. Gould expressed his regret that time would not permit him to make a personal inspection of all the great mines. He made the remark that what first attracted his attention to Tintic was an interview with Mr. Pat. Donan, reported in the Salt Lake papers, wherein Mr. Donan had said that Eureka was surrounded by mountains of silver. Mr. Gould remarked that Mr. Donan's statement did not convey the half, as there were not only mountains but valleys of silver. When informed as to the present output and future possibilities of the camp, Mr. Gould was utterly amazed, and said it was no wonder the Rio Grande Western was building into Tintic."

That is testimony from one whose eyes were never known to exaggerate the belongings of "the other fellow," and whose tongue rarely indulges in enthusiastic phrases on any subject. New as it is, Tintic is one of the world's greatest mining camps, and has in its still but half-explored mountain sides the making of a thousand millionaires. Its ores are said by experts to be almost identical with those of Leadville, and they are practically limitless in quantity.

West Tintic, in Tooele county, has fifty or more partially developed mines, all of which show fine bodies of high-grade ore; that in the Stonewall Jackson running six hundred and forty ounces of silver, and ten dollars and forty cents in gold, to the ton.

Marvelous stories of rich discoveries have recently come from Deep Creek, below Tintic; and Marysvale in Piute county, toward which the San Pete branch of the Rio Grande Western is rapidly pushing its way, bids fair to become a wonder, even in Utah. The Homestake is in ore that yields six hundred dollars to the ton in silver, both antimonial and native.

The Star group has been shipping ore eighty or ninety miles by wagon to a railroad, but its ore, yielding from one to two hundred dollars to the ton, will stand even that expensive mode of handling.

The Giles mines, six in number, show a seven-foot vein of low grade, free-milling ore. The Plata del Mina shows ore that runs nine hundred ounces of silver, and twenty-five dollars in gold, to the ton. The Triangle ore runs twenty-five ounces in silver, and twenty-five per cent. lead. The Crystal has immense bodies of carbonate and galena ore, averaging forty ounces of silver, ten dollars in gold, and thirty per cent. of lead to the ton. The Clyde and Crown Point ores run from ten to four hundred ounces of silver, and from five to fifty per cent. copper to the ton. The Antelope is getting out large quantities of ore yielding twenty ounces of silver and five dollars in gold to the ton. The region is apparently one of the richest ever discovered in the Territory, and, with the coming of the railroad, is destined to witness a tremendous mining boom.

Away down in Washington county, cornering on Nevada and Arizona, large bodies of silver ore, chiefly in the form of chlorides, have been found. There, far from railroads and the noise of "the madding crowd," two companies, the Christy and the Stormont, have worked along quietly, and taken out five million ounces of fine silver. The region has been but little explored, and there seems no reason to doubt that many valuable mines will ultimately be found among its mountains and gulches.

A wild rush has taken place, during August, 1891, to a region in Cache county, north of Ogden, where amazing discoveries of silver have just been made. A town of a thousand inhabitants sprang up in two weeks, and has been christened "La Plata," which is Spanish for "The Silver." The papers have been filled with accounts of fabulously rich strikes and finds, and if half the stories are true, an other great bonanza camp is assured. So, from its northernmost to its southernmost bounds, Utah is a mighty treasury of silver and golden opportunities and possibilities.

Utah is one of the world's bonanza-lands, a realm of realization for the dreams of gold and silver hunters, a prospectors' and miners' true El Dorado.

VII.

MISCELLANEOUS MINING.

Unlimited Variety of Utah's Mineral Resources—
Everything Found but Tin.

BUT WITH all its mighty mountain treasure-houses of royal ore, gold and silver are but two items in the long and glorious inventory of Utah's mineral wealth. Of all the metals and minerals in human use, tin is perhaps the only one not found in workable quantities within the borders of this wonderland. Run over but part of the almost endless list: Alum is found in Utah and Salt Lake counties; aluminum, in Davis and Morgan counties; antimony, in Box Elder, Piute and Garfield counties; agates, in endless quantities, and of great beauty, in Emery county; arsenic in Washington and Iron counties; bismuth, in Juab, San Pete, and Morgan counties; copper in Juab, Miller and Salt Lake counties; copperas, in Utah county; coal, exhaustless in quantity, and unsurpassed in quality, in Summit, Utah, San Pete, Emery, and Iron counties; carbonate of soda, by thousands of tons, in Salt Lake county; chalcedony and chrysolite, in various regions; cinnabar or quicksilver, in San Pete county; Fuller's earth, in many places; garnets, in Tooele county; gold, in Salt Lake, Juab, Tooele, and other counties; granite, in Salt Lake, San Pete, and every other county in the territory; graphite or plumbago, in Utah county; gypsum, in Juab, San Pete and Washington counties; iron, hematite and magnetic, in Davis, Morgan, Juab, Cache and Iron counties; jasper, in numerous places; jet, in San Pete and Emery counties; kaolin, in Utah, Salt Lake, Davis, Tooele and Sevier counties; manganese, in Utah and Tooele counties; malachite, in Juab, Beaver and several other counties; marble, of every color and the finest quality, in many localities; mica, in Davis, Salt Lake and Garfield counties; nitre, in vast quantities, in various regions; oolite, in San Pete county; opals, of many kinds, nearly everywhere; ozokerite, or mineral wax, in Utah, Wasatch and Emery counties; rock-salt, millions of tons, in Juab, San Pete, Sevier and other counties; saltpetre, in Utah county; silver in nearly if not quite every county in the territory; sulphur, enough to supply the world, in Millard, Beaver and Utah counties; topaz, white, yellow and blue, in Tooele, Box Elder and various other counties; tourmaline, in many places; talc, in Utah, Emery and Piute counties; zincblende and sulphide, in various counties; alabaster, amethysts, asbestos, asphaltum, azurite, basalt, bitumen, bog-iron, cats-eyes, epsomite, lignite, ochres of every hue, onyx, ribbon jasper, rose quartz, ruby silver, sardonyx, satin spar, specular iron, zincite and eighty-nine other metals and minerals are found in greater or less abundance all over the territory.

Thousands of square miles are underlaid by coal. Utah could supply a nation with fuel for centuries to come. At Scofield and at Castle Gate, on the Rio Grande Western Railway, the Pleasant Valley Coal Company, during 1890, mined nearly 250,000 tons of coal equal to the best Pennsylvania bituminous article. The vein at Scofield averages fourteen feet in thickness, and the mines are simply mountains of coal. At Castle Gate, the company has a hundred coke ovens, and in 1890, turned out 10,000 tons of coke, With coal unsurpassed in the world, the Castle Gate coke will ultimately be found equal to the best that Connellsville produces. The Union Pacific Company owns coal-mines at Scofield, near those of the Pleasant Valley Company, which in 1890, produced about 100,000 tons. The Home Coal Company and the Chalk Creek Company have mines near Coalville, on the Weber river, in Summit county, that produced 36,400 tons of coal in 1890. Salt Lake City used nearly 100,000 tons. One of the sights at the World's Fair in Chicago is to be a solid block of Pleasant Valley coal, twenty-eight feet thick, twenty-eight feet long, and eight feet wide. It will be bound with iron bands, carefully padded and boxed in. There are said to be in Iron county veins of solid coal a hundred feet in thickness. Iron abounds everywhere. The Tintic ore runs about sixty per cent. metallic iron, and from five to fifteen dollars in gold, to the ton. One of the most remarkable

Coke Ovens, Castle Gate

deposits of iron ore in the world is in Iron county, which takes its name from its vast beds of the most useful of all the metals. It lies in prodigious parallel belts, one of which is described as being sixteen miles long by three miles wide. Experts declare there are 500,000,000 tons in sight. It runs sixty-two per cent. metallic iron, but with a trace of sulphur and phosphorus. When that region of mineral miracles is penetrated by a railroad, as it soon will be by the Rio Grande Western, the eyes of creation will be made stick out past its hat-rim with amazement and admiration. Iron is found in all the region about Ogden, in Box Elder, Morgan, Cache, and Weber counties; and in nearly, if not quite, every other county in the territory.

Great Salt Lake would supply the world with salt, and never miss it. At Salina on the San Pete Valley branch of the Rio Grande Western Railway, there are five mountains, vast Wasatch peaks, of solid rock salt, so pure and clear that one can read through a block of it, and similar deposits are found near Nephi and in a number of other regions. The winds sometimes in a single night pile up hundreds of tons of sulphate of soda on the shores of Salt Lake; and, just below Manti on the Rio Grande Western road, are the Saleratus Beds, where for several miles the whole earth is covered with an efflorescent soda sufficiently pure for household use. Copperas, almost pure and in large quantities, has been found in Spanish Fork Canyon. Roofing slate, of unsurpassable quality, and of many colors, abounds on Antelope Island. Ozokerite, or mineral wax, has been discovered near Soldier Summit, on the Rio Grande Western Railway. It is proof against water, air and acids, and can be used to render other fabrics equally impervious. It is a perfect insulator, and is largely utilized for phonograph cylinders and cathedral candles. In its natural state it is black and waxy; when refined it becomes white and almost translucent. No ordinary heat softens it. The only other known deposit of it in the world is in Russia, and is said to have yielded $300,000,000. Gilsonite, named for the veteran prospector, Sam Gilson, who discovered it, is found in exhaustless quantities near Price Station, and in a number of other places. It is said to be ninety-nine per cent. pure asphaltum. Cowboys and hunters bring reports of a great lake of asphaltum, somewhat like that of Trinidad, in the Green River region, in which the cattle get stuck like flies on sticky fly-paper. Near Agate Station, on the Rio Grande Western Railway, are thousands of acres of superb water-agates. Some specimens five feet in diameter, flawless and beautifully tinted, have been found; and among them carnelians, one of which measured five inches across. But why go on with the enumeration? It would require a volume as big as an unabridged dictionary to hold the mere muster-roll of Utah resources and products. There is scarcely anything in all the catalogue of human needs or greeds that is not supplied in this vast Deity-made storehouse.

VIII.

BRIEFLY RETROSPECTIVE.

Utah's Progress and Possibilities — Population the Territory Could Easily Support.

SUCH is Utah, the Gem of the Rockies, where all grandeurs and glories of scene, all charms and salubrities of climate, and all riches of soil and forest and mine, unite to form one of earth's grandest garden-spots. It is a land of majestic dimensions, incomputable resources, and illimitable possibilities; a land of gold and silver mountains, of fruit-trees and vineyards, of lowing kine and golden grain; under the feet a carpet of flowers bespangled with gold-dust, and the bluest of heavens bending above and resting its arch on the walls of the Sierras.

With a population as dense as that of Ohio, seventy-five to the square mile, Utah, with 87,750 square miles of domain, would maintain 6,581,250 people. With two hundred and thirty to the square mile, as in Massachusetts, Utah would be an empire of 20,182,500 souls. It now has a population of but 220,932; so that all the great opportunities of mighty state-building still remain open to every energetic and enterprising new-comer, and the tide of brain and brawn and capital is already beginning to flow in. The assessed valuation of real and personal property rose from $51,917,312 in 1889, to $104,758,750 in 1890; an increase of nearly 102 per cent. in a single year. The banking capital increased during the same year, from $1,580,000, to $3,951,500, an increase of 150 per cent.; and the deposits rose from $5,882,213 to $9,572,286, an increase of 63 per cent. There is virtually no debt, and the total taxation is but seventeen mills on the dollar of an assessment at one-fifth valuation, or about three and one-half mills on the dollar of real value assessment. There are no delinquent taxes, and consequently no delinquent tax-lists for the newspapers. The Salt Lake County tax-list for 1890 amounted to $538,795, all of which was promptly paid, except $2,853 that represented erroneous assessments. The Salt Lake City tax-list amounted to $215,709; of which all but $1,138 was speedily paid in, and the trifling sum unpaid represented erroneous or disputed assessments. Could any statement, in so few words, give a more vivid idea of the prosperity of the region and its people? In the year ending June 30, 1890, nearly $5,000,000 was spent in new buildings; and the capitalization of the new mining, manufacturing, mercantile and miscellaneous corporations, organized in the Territory during the year, reached the enormous total of $47,932,000. There are about 1,200 miles of railroad in the Territory, and new lines are being pushed in many directions. The whole region shows the rush of improvement and prosperity.

Mountain Milk Cart

Utah's mines of gold, silver, copper and lead, in 1890, yielded $14,346,783; its farms, orchards and gardens produced $10,000,000; its flocks and herds $5,000,000; its coal, iron and other minerals $1,000,000; its lumber, salt and similar commodities $1,000,000; and its manufactories, in round numbers, $5,000,000; a grand total of $36,346,783, or about $160 for every man, woman and child, Gentile and Mormon, of its population, as the proceeds of one year's work. Where on all God's earth can a better showing be made?

Utah is the banner-land of thrift and progress.

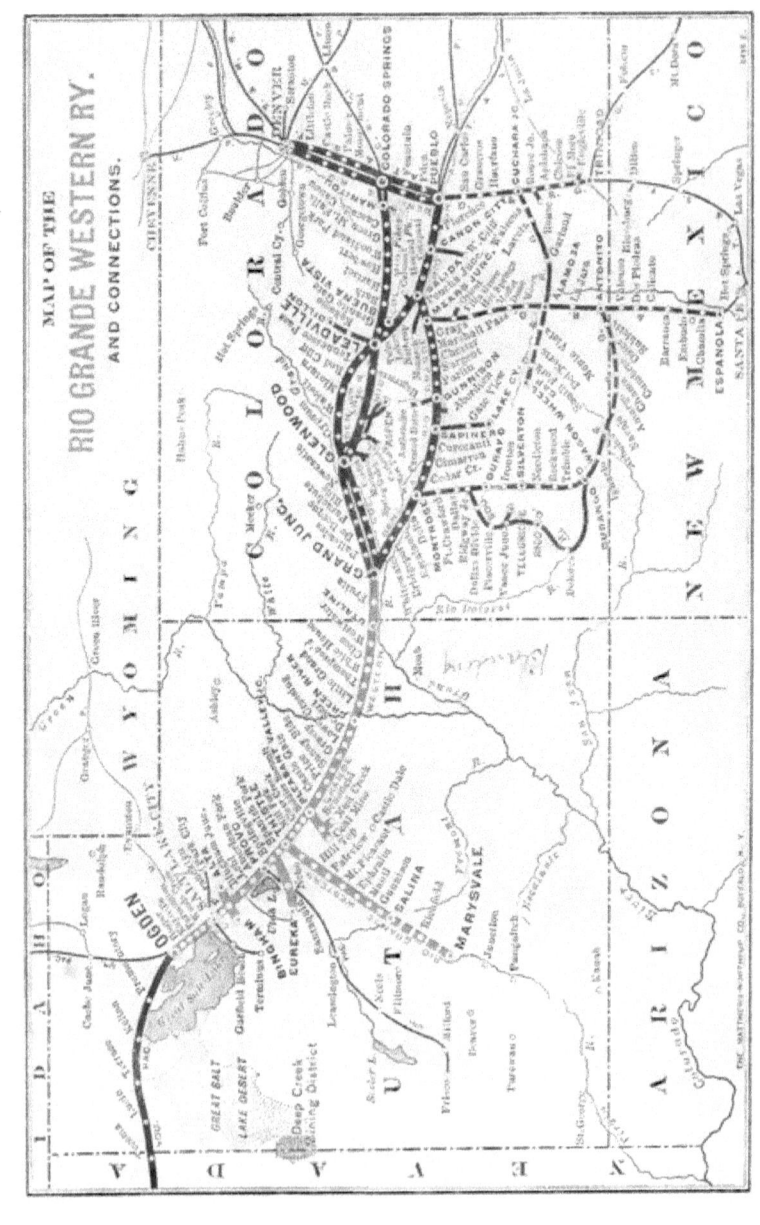

IX
UTAH'S GREAT RAILWAY.

THE GRAND HIGHWAY OF TRAVEL.

From Mountain to Meadow.

When God had reared the rugged walls
  'Round Utah's verdi vales:
Then man came on his mission and
  He laid two shining rails.
O'er which, in perfect palace cars,
  Humanity is whirled
At sixty miles an hour through
  This wonder of the world.

From frozen frigid mountains with
  Their polished peaks of snow.
To fields of waving golden grain and
  Meadowlands, below.
Through gardens in whose presence even
  Paradise would pale.
At sixty miles an hour we
  Are whirled along the rail.

OVER hundreds of miles of this magnificent young empire, opening it up to the knowledge and admiration of the outside world, to settlement and development and marvelous growth, stretches the Rio Grande Western Railway; a Utah line in every stem and branch, switch, rail and tie; a Utah line in every whirr of wheels and whoop of engine, in every interest, effort, purpose and ambition. Though it leads everywhere, and is the only route to many wondrous regions, it begins and ends in Utah, except the one long arm which reaches out to clasp hands with its eastern connections at Grand Junction. It has been a potent factor in the advancement of the territory, and has built itself by upbuilding Utah. It is one of the engineering miracles of the age. It cuts in a thousand places, the rugged backbone of the continent. It traverses regions where none but a madman, or a genius inspired, would ever have

dreamed of laying a track for even a circus trick-mule to travel. Its trains spin along where it would seem almost impossible for a mountain goat to climb, or anything without wings to pass. Its tracks double and cross themselves like the paths of a bird in the air. And yet, so perfect is its engineering, so massive and so admirable its construction, and so ceaseless the care and supervision of its every detail, that there has never been a serious accident on its lines. Its tracks of heavy steel rails, laid in many places on a bed of solid granite, are patrolled day and night by vigilant watchmen; every engine is inspected at regular intervals along the way, and every car-wheel rigidly tested. So that travel upon it is really safer than on the prairie roads of Illinois and Iowa, where accidents do now and then occur. Here — never.

The Rio Grande Western trains are as perfect and as elegant in all their appointments as the famous New York Central and Pennsylvania "Limited." Its cars, from smokers to sleepers, are models of beauty and comfort, including

Hegerman Pass

Echo Cliffs

 all the improvements of the age. Its drawing-room and sleeping-cars are massive in build, richly decorated with carving and inlaying of various-colored woods, gilding and painting, and costly mirrors and curtains, and furnished with luxurious cushions, marble wash-basins with hot and cold water, snowy towels, and every convenience of first-class hotels. The beds are as clean and comfortable as those of any hotel in New York, Philadelphia, or Chicago; and the wonder-weary traveler delightfully dreams over two hundred and fifty miles of crag and canyon, cliff, cataract, precipice and desert, without a jar or a jolt.

The day coaches on all trains are built as strongly and with as much attention to artistic effect as the sleepers or parlor-cars. Every car has neat and spacious toilet-rooms, with lavatories for men and women, and lounging and smoking rooms like those of the sleeping-cars. The mail, express and baggage cars are constructed so as to combine the greatest possible strength with the highest facilities for the speedy handling of their various freightage. All cars and platforms are brilliantly lighted by gas, which is carried in cylinders underneath. The locomotives are models of strength and ponderous beauty. Each weighs 130,000 pounds, or double the weight of the engines in general use a few years ago, and every detail of the mechanism is calculated to secure the greatest attainable power, speed and safety. The entire effect is that of a flying train of palaces-on-wheels, where every man is a sovereign and every woman is a queen —who holds either a first or second class ticket. There are no changes of cars between Chicago, Denver, Salt Lake, Ogden and San Francisco, except for passengers who wish to take in the magnificent scenery along the Denver & Rio Grande narrow-gauge line. They change at Grand Junction by simply stepping from one car to another at the union depot.

To the traveler on business or for pleasure, going from east to west or west to east, the Rio Grande Western Railway offers the only through line from Denver to Salt Lake City that traverses the grand scenery of the Colorado mountains and canyons, and gives choice of three famous routes: By the Denver & Rio Grande standard gauge through the Grand River canyons, and by Leadville, Colorado Springs, Pike's Peak and the Mount of the Holy Cross, by the Denver & Rio Grande narrow gauge through the Black Canyon of the Gunnison, over Marshall Pass, and through the Royal Gorge and the Grand Canyon of the Arkansas; and by the Colorado Midland, by Glenwood Springs, Hagerman Tunnel, South Park, Ute Park, Pike's Peak and Manitou. To the freight shipper it offers as short a line and as quick time as any other road, with choice of seven direct connections at Denver, Colorado Springs and Pueblo: the Chicago, Burlington & Quincy, the Rock Island, the Atchison, Topeka & Santa Fé, the Missouri Pacific, Union

Pacific, Kansas Pacific, and the Union Pacific, Denver & Gulf. To anybody and everybody, bound from anywhere to anywhere else, to transcontinental tourists, as well as to local shippers and journeyers, the Rio Grande Western Railway, controlled and managed by able, progressive and liberal men, who stand in the front rank of their profession, offers every inducement and accommodation — safe track, superb trains, good service, dainty eating-houses, quick time, close connections and low rates. It is the business man's route between the West and East. It is the artist's and tourist's route to all that is sublimest and grandest in scenery on the continent. It is the sportsman's route to mountains and forests that abound with bears, cougars or mountain lions, deer, wolves and other game ; and lakes and streams that swarm with speckled trout. In one region along the line Milton Lyon and his partner, old trappers, during the early months of 1891 killed thirty-five bears, including black, cinnamon and grizzly, and a number of cougars, besides all other game : they brought in eleven bear skins to the station in one day. It is the homeseeker's route to millions on millions of acres of free farming and grazing lands. It is the stock-raiser's route to cattle-ranges and sheep-pastures that cost nothing, where the grass never dies, and the horizon is the only fence. It is the fortune-hunter's route to ten thousand bonanza mines, present and to come. It is the invalid's route to one of God's own sanitariums, where every breath is balm, and health is universal as the blessed air of heaven.

All aboard for a flying trip along its lines.

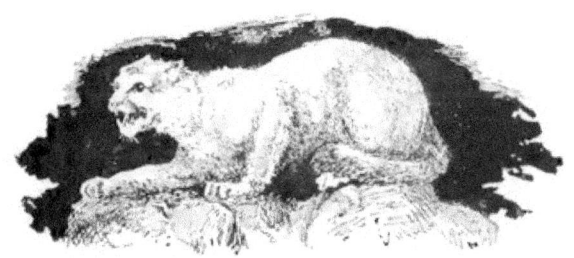

X.

A WONDERFUL TOUR.

A FLYING TRIP OVER THE LINES OF THE RIO GRANDE WESTERN, WITH GLIMPSES OF THE COUNTRY.

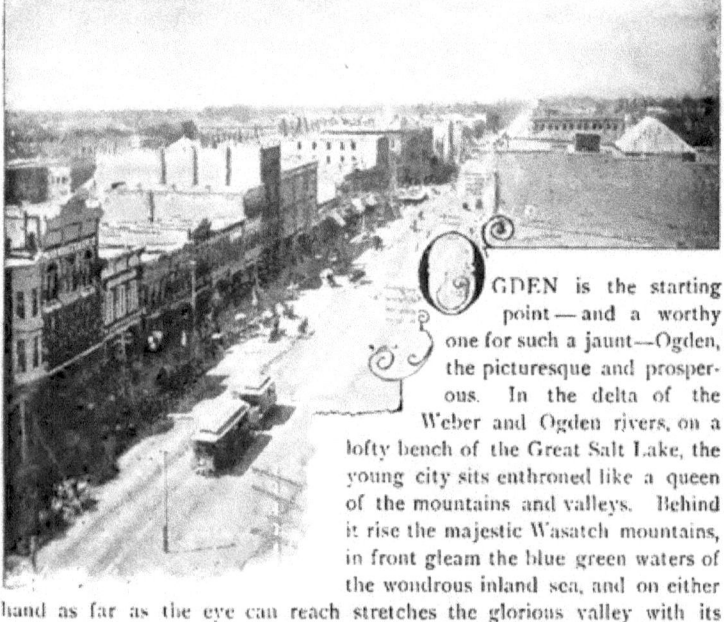

OGDEN is the starting point — and a worthy one for such a jaunt — Ogden, the picturesque and prosperous. In the delta of the Weber and Ogden rivers, on a lofty bench of the Great Salt Lake, the young city sits enthroned like a queen of the mountains and valleys. Behind it rise the majestic Wasatch mountains, in front gleam the blue green waters of the wondrous inland sea, and on either hand as far as the eye can reach stretches the glorious valley with its grain-fields and meadows, its orchards and vineyards, gardens and groves. Ogden grew from a population of 6,069, in 1880, to 14,919, in 1890, an increase of 129 per cent., and it has nearly 20,000 in 1891. Its eighty wholesale houses did $7,181,000 of business in 1890, and its bank clearings ran from $250,000 to $500,000 a week. Its real estate transfers during the year reached the amazing aggregate of $9,978,277, or nearly $850,000 a month, and 1,037 buildings were erected at a cost of $1,769,719. Its factories increased over 50 per cent., and the year's product amounted to $1,538,430. It has seven banks with a combined capital of about $1,500,000. Its post-office handled 4,745,000 letters, and its telegraph offices 1,422,696 messages during 1890, a record hardly equaled in any other city in the world of the same population. Ogden has water works with a capacity

of 10,000,000 gallons a day, twenty miles of electric street railway, electric light, gas works and telephone. It has many costly and handsome public and private buildings, fine public schools and private academies, including a military institute. The territorial reform school is also located here. The who'e surrounding country is rich in mines of gold, silver, copper, lead and iron, and the newly discovered bonanzas of La Plata are almost at the doors of Ogden. The famous Utah Hot Springs, where many marvelous cures have been effected, are near the city, and a charming bathing resort on the Salt Lake beach is in plain view of the court-house. Ogden is growing and improving at race-horse speed, and is destined to become one of the most important cities between the Missouri river and the Pacific coast. From its magnificent union depot, surpassing anything of the kind in Omaha, Minneapolis, St. Paul or St. Louis, the superb Rio Grande Western train rolls out for Denver and the east.

A rush of eighteen miles, through fields waving with rich harvests and orchards bending under their burdens of fruit, through Hooper and Layton, and it passes Kaysville where two Mormon farmers recently raised a hundred and six bushels of wheat to the acre and sold it, measuring that number of bushels for every acre they had in cultivation, to the great Zion store in Salt Lake City. Four miles further to Farmington, where the spur of track runs down to the Lake Park Bathing Beach with its pavilions and piers, bathhouses, verandas and promenades, and its extensive salt works; on past Lake Shore Station, where tens of thousands of tons of salt are made without cost from the wondrous lake waters; past Wood's Crossing and Hot Springs, where a flood of almost boiling waters pours from the side of a granite cliff, as full of healing virtues as those of Arkansas or Carlsbad or Baden Baden; on amid meadows of sweet-scented alfalfa and orchards of peaches and apricots, nectarines, apples and plums, with the grand Wasatch peaks always on the left hand and the azure expanse of the great lake on the right; and, with a shrill "howdye-do" of salutation from the locomotive to the spires and minarets of Zion, the train dashes into Salt Lake City, the capital of Utah and of Mormondom.

With engine fresh coaled and watered and wheels all newly inspected, it sweeps on between long avenues of shade trees and past charming suburban homes embowered in foliage, fruit and flowers, and seven miles out it begins to pass the great smelters at Francklyn, Germania and Bingham Junction strung along the track for four miles. They reduce about 75,000 tons of silver ores a year.

At Bingham Junction, one branch line strikes off to the rich Bingham mines sixteen miles southwest. Another branch, ten miles long, runs to Wasatch at the mouth of Little Cottonwood Canyon, where all the white granite for the Mormon temple in Salt Lake City was quarried. For four miles on both sides the canyon is walled with this beautiful stone. From Wasatch a tramway leads to Alta where the famous Emma mine is located.

The main line train halts but an instant at Bingham Junction, and speeds on up the fertile and beautiful Jordan River Valley, past Draper and Jordan Narrows, and after a run of twenty-one miles whirs into Lehi, a beautiful little city of 3,000 people, with all its houses hidden in the green of trees and vines. It takes its name from Lehi, according to The Book of Mormon, the ancestor of the American Indians. The country around it is like a vast garden. Within from twenty to forty-five miles are all the mines of Cottonwood, American Fork, Bingham and Tintic. There are a number of flourishing manufactories, and the Utah Beet Sugar Factory, is the largest concern

of the kind in the United States, the plant costing nearly $500,000. Near here, where the Jordan River flows out of Utah Lake, are hot springs of great curative power.

On four miles to American Fork, a pretty town of 2,500 people, the whole place, like every other in this region, lost in fruit-trees and flowers. Near it, on the shores of beautiful Utah Lake, is a favorite picnic and camping ground. A $20,000 hotel has recently been built. Here start the wagon roads to American Fork mines, about twenty miles away. Four miles further and Battle Creek is passed, and a further whirl of nine miles brings Provo into view — and a charming view it is. A city of 5,000 people, on the shores of the lovely Utah Lake, with the mighty wall of the Wasatch mountains as a background. Handsome buildings, all buried in their wealth of fruit-trees, flowers and vines. A surrounding country that is a vast garden, teeming with every variety of grain, fruit and vegetable. Here is the largest woolen mill west of the Missouri River. Its goods are sold in nearly every state and territory of the Union; one of the leading business-houses of Salt Lake City sells no goods but those made here. The territorial insane asylum, which stands on a high point in the edge of the place, would do credit architecturally to any city of any state. Brigham Young Academy, just completed, is a large and handsome structure. Provo, during 1890, spent $360,791 in new buildings. Two daily papers are published in the city, and here the Rio Grande Western Railway crosses the Utah Central.

On, with a whirr of flying wheels, six miles to Springville, where the Tintic Range branch of the Rio Grande Western leaves the main line, and pushes through Spanish Fork, a city of 3,500 people in "a land flowing with milk and honey," where every acre is a garden. The city put nearly $60,000 in new buildings in 1890, has flouring mills, a foundry, broom-factory and artesian wells, and is solidly prosperous in all its industries. Vast deposits of pure alum have been found here.

On through Payson and Goshen, a region rich in all agricultural productions. West of Goshen, the new branch line enters Piñon Canyon, and runs for ten miles through as wild and rugged scenes as can be found in all this region of scenic wonders. The track through the canyon is a dizzy puzzle in engineering. It winds and climbs, twists, turns and wriggles, and at last absolutely crosses itself backward and forward, tying itself into a loop like a double bow-knot. There are but two similar track tangles in the United States, one in California and the other in Colorado. Out of this canyon labyrinth, the line emerges in the far-famed Tintic mining-camp; and, just on beyond that, will doubtless ere long rush its iron-horse into the newly discovered Deep Creek bonanza region, whose richness is attracting wide-spread attention now.

Springville, where this digression left the main line, is a shade-embowered city of 3,500 population, surrounded by a region as rich and productive as the sun shines on. All grains, grasses, fruits and vegetables grow in endless profusion. Streams of limpid water flow through the

Castle Gate.

streets. About $30,000 was expended in 1890 in new buildings, and the sales of merchandise amounted to nearly $450,000. There are many creditable buildings, public and private, and a number of flourishing industries, including an extensive woolen-mill.

On four miles, to Vista and through Pole Canyon; and, in a few minutes, Castilla Springs, with its floods of healing waters, bursting from the mountain's side, is reached. There are baths of all sorts and temperatures, and a great swimming pool, and any disease that is curable by thermal waters can be relieved here.

A brief run and Thistle Junction is reached, where the San Pete Valley branch of the Rio Grande Western starts toward the vast mines and quarries, grainfields and fruit gardens that lie toward the south. Glance for a moment down this branch line. Two miles from Thistle is Asphaltum station, where there is a bed of nearly pure asphaltum, covering a square mile, and from eight to fourteen feet thick. Six miles further, and at Nebo a view is caught of Mount Nebo, one of the tallest and grandest peaks in Utah, snow-capped all the year. About a mile below Nebo the road enters the Indian Reservation, and six miles onward is Indianola, around which cluster the adobe houses and tepees of a branch of the great Ute tribe, whence Utah has its name. They do a little farming and stock-raising, and a good deal of hunting and fishing, and, all things considered, are generally doing well. Whirling on through twenty miles of pastures and farms, past Hilltop and Milburn, at Fairview a glorious view of the San Pete valley, "the granary of Utah," bursts upon the enchanted eye. The whole country for fifty miles is a mingling of field and garden. Only two miles more, and the train sweeps into Mount Pleasant, nestled in peach and apricot, apple, pear and plum trees, all bowed down with their loads of fruit. The town stands at the foot of the mountain on a commanding site. It has about 3,000 population, a flouring-mill and planing mill, and is the seat of Wasatch Academy, a Presbyterian school of some repute. Five miles in twelve minutes, and Spring City is passed, with great masses of snow-crowned mountains east and southeast of it; and, in ten miles more, Ephraim's bowers of fruit and shade are entered. In a population of 2,200, there are 800 school children, besides all those too young for schooling. A new depot, new hotel and many other new buildings tell the story of prosperity.

A dash of six miles onward, and Manti is reached, with 2,300 people, and hardly a poor man among them. Here, at the top of four lofty terraces hewn from the mountain side, stands the magnificent Mormon temple, which has cost $2,500,000, and is only second to the one in Salt Lake City. It is nearly two hundred feet long, one hundred wide and one hundred high, with massive towers at each end rising one hundred and seventy-five feet in the air. It is built of snow-white oolite, quarried out of the site on which it stands, and the whole workmanship is exquisite. It can be plainly seen for

forty miles up and down the valley. A hot spring, on the edge of the town, pours out a hundred cubic feet a minute of water gifted with remarkable medicinal qualities. Just below Manti are the strange "Saleratus Beds," where for two miles or more the road runs through vast deposits of soda pure enough for cooking purposes. It was near Manti that a railroad right-of-way man came across a Mormon Mr. Olson, who had four wives, all named Anna. The deeds to the right-of-way had to be signed by the entire four Mrs. Anna Olsons.

The train rushes on through a continuous succession of grainfields and orchards. Sterling, Gunnison and Willow Creek are passed, the Sevier Valley is entered, and the locomotive screams its greeting to Salina, the present terminus of the branch. Just back of the town are mountains of rock salt, much of it as clear as crystal, and absolutely pure. Millions on millions of tons of it can be blasted out as cheap as dirt. About a mile south of these mountainous monuments to the memory of Lot's wife is a mountain of almost pure gypsum, and there is kaolin enough to furnish all the potteries and candy-makers of the world. The whole region abounds with game and fish.

From Salina, a stage-ride, that condenses in a few hours grandeur and variety and novelty enough to glorify all the memories of the most monotonous and commonplace life, takes one into the great canyons of the Colorado, where God Almighty Himself seems to have finished His labors in scenic magnificence, feeling that there was nothing more for even Omnipotence to do for the delight of human eye and soul. In Marble Canyon, the walls of solid marble, beautiful as ever sculptor's chisel wrought into an immortality of genius, tower thousands on thousands of feet heavenward on either hand; and along the Vermillion Cliffs, the rainbow itself fades, by contrast with the myriads of dazzling tints and hues, into a colorless arch of shamefaced fog.

The San Pete Valley which begins about thirty miles north of Manti, extends for fifty miles southward, an unbroken vision of fertility and beauty. Six miles north of Salina it merges into the glorious valley of the Sevier, which runs forty miles south to the mouth of Clear Creek Canyon, leading to the new and much-talked-of Marysvale mines. Below Marysvale begins another valley of wonderful wealth, that extends to the cotton and semi-tropical fruit lands of Southern Utah. Is the Rio Grande Western going to push its long arms of iron and steel into these new empires of rich fruitage and freightage? It would be safe to lay wagers upon it.

But back to Thistle, to resume the interrupted main line jaunt. Thistle has immense quantities of fine building stone. On, amid crags and canyons; through Red Narrows, Mill Fork and Clear Creek; past Soldier Summit, where one of Albert Sidney Johnston's soldiers in the "Mormon War" lies buried nearly 10,000 feet above the level of the sea. Near Soldier Summit, ozokerite or mineral wax is found. Seven miles further, and Pleasant Valley

Junction is reached, whence a branch road, eighteen miles in length, leads to the Pleasant Valley coal-mines, where hundreds of thousands of tons of black diamonds are annually mined. At Hale's station on the coal branch, nine miles from the Junction, the Rio Grande Western company cuts all its supplies of ice on Fish creek, a stream clear as crystal and swarming with trout.

From Pleasant Valley Junction to Kyune on the main line is six miles, and the whole distance is through mountains of the finest quality of gray sandstone, which several strong companies are quarrying and shipping. The name of Kyune originated with a shiftless fellow who, in hunting, some years ago, came across "a strange varmint" where the station now stands. He described it as a "kind of a ky-une lookin' critter," meaning a sort of cross between a coyote and a coon — and the name stuck. On, nine miles through the glorious canyon of Price river, where every turn of the track reveals scenes but little less grand and picturesque than those of the Grand Canyon of the Arkansas. Precipices of stone, thousands of feet high, carved and twisted, by ages of floods and storms, into all weird and fantastic shapes that the maddest imagination can conceive; castles, cathedrals, fortresses, towers and spires, animals, birds and reptiles, all on a scale so colossal that the mightiest structures of men are dwarfed, by contrast — for comparison there is none — to sick children's Noah's Arks, with elephants an inch high and giraffes scarcely larger than full-grown Jersey mosquitoes. The flying train passes out of the canyon at Castle Gate, where two gigantic pillars of stone, towering nearly to the clouds, form a gateway that has been pictured by artists and daubers throughout the world. Here are the great Castle Gate coal-mines and coking-works, which have already been mentioned. Three miles eastward is Helper station, where a "helper" engine is attached to trains coming west to help them over the steep grades of Price Canyon.

Seven miles onward to Price Station, where Price river is crossed. It is the shipping point for all the country within a hundred and fifty miles of the road on the

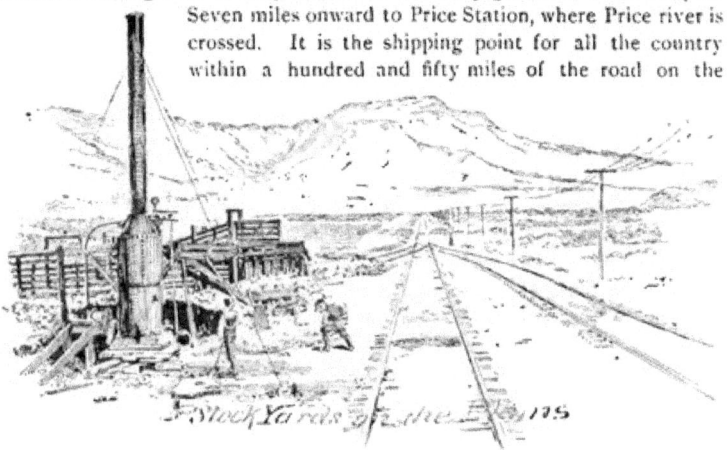

Stock Yards of the Plains.

north, including two Indian Reservations and a military post, Fort Thornburg; and for a region extending for fifty miles south of the town. It handles a great deal of live stock, and ships the asphaltum of the Fort Duchesne company. It is the starting point of daily stage lines to many places north and south of the railroad, and boasts of a lively newspaper as one of its pet institutions. On through Huntington and Farnham, a twelve-mile-long strip of green fertility about two miles wide, walled in by desert. Wherever water touches the soil, trees, .rich harvest-fields, meadows of alfalfa, grass waist-high to the cattle, fruit and flowers. Sunnyside is a narrow oasis. At Cedar the whole desert as far as the eye can reach is dotted with straggling clumps of Spanish cedar or mountain mahogany, which grows in some mysterious way where even sagebrush gives up disheartened. "Grassy," seven miles further east, seems to take its name from the fact that there is not a blade of grass within a mile of it. Lower Crossing of Price river is a stock-shipping point. About twenty-five miles away in the wild Book Mountains begins the Range Valley, eighty miles long by fifteen wide, wonderfully fertile and watered by mountain streams, but absolutely inaccessible except by a hazardous mule or burro trail. It is used by the Range Valley Cattle Company as a ranch, said to be the most extensive in Utah. The whole region abounds with bear, deer, mountain lions or cougars, lynxes, wolves and other game, and all the streams swarm with speckled trout. Six miles further east is Green River Station, one of the prettiest spots on the whole line, an oasis of verdure and bloom in a wide-spreading desert. It is just west of the long bridge over Green river. The Rio Grande Western has an elegant hotel here, called the Palmer House, in honor of the president of the company. It is surrounded by green lawns, shade-trees, gardens and fruit. Fountains play in a charming little park in front of the house, although every drop of water has to be piped and pumped from the river. The house is admirably kept, and its table is not surpassed at any railroad station in the country.

Eight miles east of Green River, "Solitude" is well named. On through nineteen miles of desert, the only semblance of green is an occasional patch of dwarfed and brownish sage-brush. It is so bare and barren that it would seem as though the very ravens that solemnly stalk around amid its desolation would have to carry their own canteens and haversacks, as Phil. Sheridan said the crows would have to do in the Shenandoah Valley. And yet there is a wondrous fascination about it. There is a suggestion of the Great Sahara. Lew Wallace's marvelous description of the desert in "Ben Hur" rises before the eye of memory. And then this American desert is walled in on both sides by such weirdly, wondrously fantastic mountains that it is always interesting to the point of fascination. In some places the cliffs that border it are first low, bare mounds; then higher ranges level along the top; then mighty precipices striped horizontally with white, yellow, dark-red and purple strata, the layers as regular as though painted, and the vast masses cut by deep canyons into millions of strange shapes. Near Lower Crossing, off to the eastward, there is a figure of an elephant five hundred feet long lying down, with feet, legs, ears and trunk as perfect as though hewn by Titanic sculptors. In the same region, on a terraced foundation a thousand feet high, there is a vast temple a half mile long and five hundred feet high, with a mighty dome in the centre rising two hundred feet higher; while away off, ten or fifteen miles west, there is a far larger structure, double domed, one dome being pyramidal and the other conical. Between Crescent and Thompson's, away off to the west or southwest, looms up a great city of red sandstone on top of a lofty mountain. Buildings, chimneys, towers and spires are all so perfect that it is almost impossible to believe that the genii or the fairies have not reared a real city as large at least as Chicago in this wild realm of fantasy. Twenty-five miles away, on the top of a lofty mountain range, stands an exact counterpart of the Capitol at Washington that must be a mile in length and from five hundred to a thousand feet in height to show as it does at so great a distance.

Thompson's Springs, twenty-seven miles east of Green River, is another oasis of trees and grass, grain and flowers. The water is piped four miles from a spring in the canyon. The place is a shipping-point for cattle from the distant ranches. There is abundance of coal and asphaltum in the neighborhood, but neither has ever been worked. On through the mountain-walled desert, past Sager's and Whitehouse and Cisco; and Agate is reached, where thousands of acres are covered with beautiful water-agates and carnelians. Cottonwood is passed, and at Westwater the train plunges into one of the wildest and grandest canyons on the line. For fifteen miles of wonder Nature seems to have cut her weirdest capers. Between Westwater and Utaline, across Grand River, along the dizzy brink of which the train is flying, is a vast cavern in a blood-red cliff. It seems a fit temple for the mighty gods and other queeriosities, whose giant effigies, carved in granite and red sandstone, stand in solemn, silent array along a thousand strange cliffs and mountain-tops. Near Utaline, where the Rio Grande Western, for the only time in all its wanderings, crosses the boundary-line of Utah, and enters Colorado, off far to the southward, through a break in the wall of mountains, another range appears, crowned with a hundred or more gigantic copies of the Great Pyramid of Ghizeh, magnified a score of times. Across the river near Ruby, on the point of a mountain sits a huge Arab, with a dark-stained red sandstone face, and a white stone turban and burnous; while behind him stands a perfect dromedary two hundred feet high, with stony eyes apparently fixed upon his mighty master. Not more than a mile away, a procession of gigantic Egyptian priests, robed and garlanded, are marching down the precipice, the smallest of them a hundred feet tall. Past Ruby, and the canyon opens out into desert again, bounded

Sangre de Cristo, in thy cold purity
Thou'rt emblematic of blood shed to free
The world of its woe for man's soul's security,
Shed to save sin-fettered mortals like me.

Sangre de Cristo,
Bright monte vista,
Thy cloud piercing peaks
Shall my monument be;
And when I am sleeping
Where thy shades are creeping
Sangre de Cristo,
Will thou shelter me?

Marshall Pass and Mt. Ouray

Pikes Peak, through the Garden of the Gods.

Loch Ivanhoe.

Up near the mountain's craggy crest.
 The mighty moguls strong and proud:
 The snow drifts beating 'gainst their breast
  With pointed pilots pierce the cloud.
 High mountains - seeming little hills -
  Emboss the spreading plain below.
 And rivers look like laughing rills
  As down the distant vale they flow.

Here in a wierd cold wintry grave
 Wrapped in a marble shroud of snow.
With not a ripple not a wave
 Calmly sleeps Loch Ivanhoe.
But with the coming of the spring
 The little flowers will bud and blow
And gladsome songs the birds will sing.
 Along the banks of Ivanhoe.

on both sides still by the mountains swarming with weird, fantastic shapes.
The train flies on past Crevasse; and Fruita, where water's magical touch
has transformed the desert into a garden of flowers and fruit, and made the
station a great shipping-point of peaches, apricots, apples, pears and melons.
Roan is left behind, and in a few minutes more Grand Junction is reached.
It is a city of about 4,000 people, tastefully laid out and well built. It has
electric light, Holly water-works, street-cars, good schools, churches of all the
leading denominations, and daily papers chuck-full of boom spirit. Just
back of the city, the whole face of the mountains assumes the exact shape of
vast white-stone curtains, a thousand feet long, fluted and plaited, and surmounted by quaintly carved iambrequins of red sandstone fifty or a hundred
feet high. Grand Junction, as its name denotes, is a junctional point of
both rivers and railroads. Here the Grand and the Gunnison rivers unite;
and here the east-bound journeyer has choice of three routes, all abounding
in magnificent scenery, world-famous mines of gold and silver, glorious
health and pleasure resorts, and unsurpassed hunting and fishing; and all
superbly equipped, and furnishing every comfort, convenience and luxury,
that the highest perfection of railroading can suggest.

1. The Denver & Rio Grande standard-gauge line whirls him through
all the wild glories of the Grand River Canyons; and past the famous Rock
Creek, Red Cliff and Belden mines, which in rugged picturesqueness surpass
the dizziest habitations of Alpine cliff-dwellers. It takes him through Leadville, one of the mining wonders of the ages; a camp 12,000 feet above the
low level of the sea, that in ten years produced nearly $160,000,000 in gold,
silver, copper and lead; and that turned out $13,684,000 in 1889. It spins
him through the Grand Canyon of the Arkansas and the Royal Gorge, that
all human language has been bankrupted trying to describe; past Colorado
Springs, where a beautiful young city of 12,000 people has risen, like a
magic exhalation, in a day, around wondrous fountains of healing; under
the shadows of Pike's Peak, with its crown of everlasting snow, and its
marvelous cogwheel railroad, a trip over which is worthy of a century's
remembrance; and into Denver, the proud "Queen City of the Rocky
Mountains," whose history lays all romance flat upon its back, and makes
the most gorgeous tales of genii and fairies seem commonplace and tame.

2. Or, from Grand Junction, the traveler can take the far-famed Denver & Rio Grande narrow-gauge line, which condenses in a four-hundred-and-twenty-five mile run grand and varied scenery enough to have rendered
the world picturesque, if God Almighty had made it everywhere else a
desert plain. The savage grandeur and beauty of the Black Canyon of the
Gunnison; of Marshall Pass, where the road winds sixty-five miles to travel
thirteen, and where one can look back over eight tracks, all at different
heights; of the Grand Canyon of the Arkansas and the Royal Gorge, defy
all genius of tongue or pen, brush or pencil to depict them.

3. Last, but far from least in interest or importance, the Colorado Midland, with a superb track, and trains perfect in every detail, will send the eastward-journeying pilgrim flying from Grand Junction, past Glenwood Springs, with its glorious fountains and baths; through Red Rock Canyon; past the majestic Seven Castles; through Hell Gate, with its labyrinth of savage grotesqueries; past exquisite Loch Ivanhoe, a liquid jewel on the rocky bosom of giant ruggedness; and through Hagerman Tunnel, 11,528 feet, or more than two miles above the level of the sea, leaving great masses of snowy clouds far below. The train speeds on through Leadville and Buena Vista; winds around Gold Hill, where Bierstadt sketched his great picture, "The Heart of the Rocky Mountains;" dashes through South Park, Granite Canyon and Summit Park; past picturesque and beautiful Green Mountain Falls, a fashionable summer saunteringplace; around the foot of Pike's Peak; past the Garden of the Gods; through Manitou, with its famous springs and caverns, its half-hundred hotels and its swarms of summer guests from every region of the globe; through Colorado Springs; and into Denver — into whose royal borders, as into those of Imperial Rome, "all roads lead"— in the Rocky Mountain Realms.

It is a trip to be remembered with profit and delight as long as life and memory last, even though one should live to discount Methuselah as a kitten. It is an unbroken eight-hundred-mile-long panorama of all that is grandest and weirdest, most sublime and beautiful in Nature's handiwork; Jehovah's artistic masterpieces on the most stupendous scale. Mountains, whose heads are crowned with the snows of untold ages, while their feet are lost in the verdure and bloom of everlasting summer gardens. Rocks, thousands on thousands of feet high, and of every tint and hue, from white and black and brown to pink and blue, golden, orange and blood-red, carved and chiseled by the omnipotent fingers of whirlpools and eddies and rushing floods into gigantic sculptures that dwarf all the sphynxes and pyramids, obelisks, arches, domes and towers of men to puny babies' playthings. Mighty rivers, as large as the upper Mississippi or Ohio, tumbling and plunging and kicking up their liquid heels like the maddest and giddiest trout brooks. Peaks, whose crests are wreathed with snowy clouds; and canyons, whose fathomless, yawning glooms lay an unwonted spell of decent silence

on even the most flippant average fashionable tourist gazer. Cataracts and cascades, whose wild, leaping waters are churned and dashed into foam and spray and feathery mist long before they strike the stony basins dizzy depths below; while myriads of irises and rainbows dance in every gorge where a straggling sunbeam finds its lucent way. And deserts weird and desolate as the Great Sahara, looking as though the ocean had been swept by a million cyclones and whirlwinds, and in the midst of the awful commotion had suddenly petrified in eternal loneliness of alkali and sand.

All the boasted mountain scenery, from the New Hampshire " Notch " to far-famed " Lookout," where the historic " Battle above the Clouds " never took place, would look like ant-hills and pig-troughs in any hundred miles of the Utah and Colorado Rockies—the only Real Wonderland, with the " R. W." blown in the glass, of the United-Statian part of the new world. Compared with a thousand places along the Rio Grande Western route, all such much-advertised scenes as the Horseshoe Curve, the Bridge across the Potomac at Harper's Ferry, the New River Rapids and the Hawk's Nest, and the would-be wildest little Adirondack crags and glens and gullies, grow tame as tennis courts or croquet grounds. All the rocks and ripples, cliffs and gulches of the 20,000-annual-visitored Dells of the Wisconsin could be lost beyond the power of the keenest-eyed buzzard that wears feathers to find them in this land of Vast Picturesques. The whole Alleghany and Blue Ridge systems of mountains would look like a prairie-dog town anywhere among the glacier-capped Sierras of Utah and Colorado. The Alps themselves would dwindle by contrast. For miles at a stretch every foot of the railroad track had to be blasted from the solid granite face of precipices that touch the clouds, along the dizzifying margin of savage torrents that have raged and roared and foamed for ages in vain attempts to cleave for themselves a broader pathway to the far-off seas. The Rio Grande Western trains are often wrapped in clouds, and sometimes fly along for miles above the fleecy flounces of the skies; but the track, like the house of the scriptural wise man, is " builded on a rock," and *it is absolutely safe*. It never had an accident, and with its perfect system of track and car and engine inspection, it probably never will. It is The Grand Safe and Scenic Route of the World

XI.

GREAT SALT LAKE.

The Dead Sea of America — A Watery Magazine of Infinite Riches — Incomparable Sea Bathing.

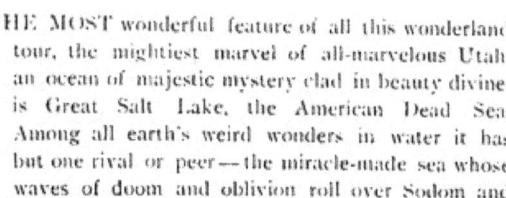

HE MOST wonderful feature of all this wonderland tour, the mightiest marvel of all-marvelous Utah, an ocean of majestic mystery clad in beauty divine, is Great Salt Lake, the American Dead Sea. Among all earth's weird wonders in water it has but one rival or peer — the miracle-made sea whose waves of doom and oblivion roll over Sodom and Gomorrah, the Chicagos of forty centuries ago. Think of a lake from twenty-five hundred to three thousand square miles in area, lying a thousand miles inland, at an altitude of four thousand, two hundred and fifty feet above the sea level, whose waters are six times as salt as those of the ocean; and, while it has no outlet, four large rivers pouring their ceaseless floods of fresh water into it without raising its mysterious surface a fraction of an inch, or ever diminishing, so far as chemical analysis can determine, its indescribable saltiness. Where does all the water go? Where does all the salt, that no streams can freshen, come from? Where are the vast saline magazines from which it draws its everlasting supplies? One may stand upon its shores and ask a thousand such questions but no answer comes from its mysterious depths, in which nothing lives but death and silence.

When, in February, 1846, twenty thousand Mormons, under the leadership of Brigham Young, started from Nauvoo, Illinois, on their two-thousand-mile pilgrimage through the trackless wilderness of the American West, they proclaimed themselves the modern Israel in search of the promised land. It was a strange fate, or destiny, or Providence, that led them to a region so similar to the "Land of Promise" of Israel of old. There, the lake of Gennesaret, or sea of Galilee, was fresh water and full of fish. The Jordan River flowed out of it and emptied into the Dead Sea, which is so salt and acrid that no living thing is found in its waters. Here, Provo or Utah Lake is fresh and sweet, and its limpid waters swarm with speckled trout and other fish as savory as any that strained the nets of Peter, James and John. Out of it flows the Mormon River Jordan, and after rambling for forty or fifty miles through orchards and meadows, grain fields and gardens, pours its silvery tide into Great Salt Lake, the saltiest body of water on the globe, surpassing even its Judean counterpart by one and a half per cent. In the Holy Land the Jordan flows from north to south, while the Utah Jordan flows from south to north. Mount Nebo stood like a giant sentinel overlooking the ancient "land flowing with milk and honey," and here Mount Nebo, lifting its crown of eternal snow twelve thousand feet heavenward, stands guard forever over a fairer Canaan than Moses viewed, but never entered.

Salt Lake was once as large as Lake Huron, and was over a thousand feet deep. Its former benches and the marks of its olden wave-plashings are as plain upon the mountain-benches as though traced but yesterday. It is now about a hundred miles long, with an average width of from twenty-five to thirty miles. It is from fifty to sixty miles wide in some places, and its greatest depth is about sixty feet. Its waters contain eighteen per cent. of solid matter, mostly salt and soda, with small proportions of sulphur, magnesia, calcium, chlorine, bromine, potassium, lithia and boracic acid. The Asiatic Dead Sea water contains twenty-three per cent. of solids, including less salt and soda and much more magnesia, calcium and potassium than Salt Lake. Atlantic Ocean water holds but 3.5 per cent. of solid material, of which salt constitutes 2.6 per cent. Hundreds of thousands of tons of salt are made by natural evaporation along the shores of the lake, and at one place near Salt Lake City a windy night never fails to pile up many tons of soda, eliminated by the movement of the waves.

Compared with this vast liquid treasure-house of riches, the greatest bonanza mines of Utah or of the United States dwindle to blind beggars' penny boxes. Take out your pencil and do a little figuring. Figures, it is said, will not lie, and you will soon find yourself standing dumfounded before your own mathematical truths.

Say Salt Lake is a hundred miles long, and has an average width of 27 miles; that gives an area of 2,700 square miles. There are 27,878,400 square feet in a mile; so the lake has an area of 75,271,680,000 square feet. Take 20 feet as its average depth; then 20 times 75,271,680,000 will give us 1,505,433,600,000 cubic feet as the contents of the lake. Now 16⅔ per cent., or one-sixth of this, according to the analysis of eminent chemists, is salt and sulphate of soda.

That is, the lake contains 250,905,600,000 cubic feet of salt and sulphate of soda. Of this vast mass one eighth is sulphate of soda and seven-eighths common salt. So there are of Na_2SO_4, or sulphate of soda, 31,363,200,-000 cubic feet; and of $NaCl$, or common salt, 219,542,400,000 cubic feet.

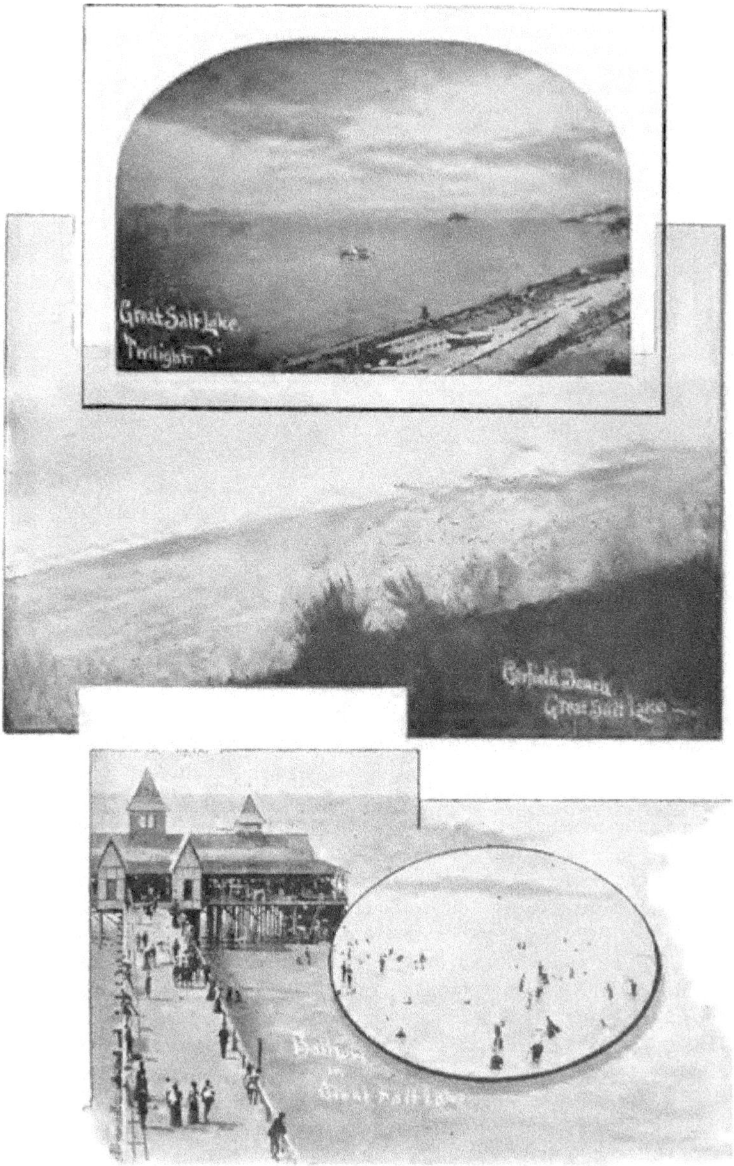
Great Salt Lake.
Twilight.
Garfield Beach
Great Salt Lake
Bathing
in
Great Salt Lake

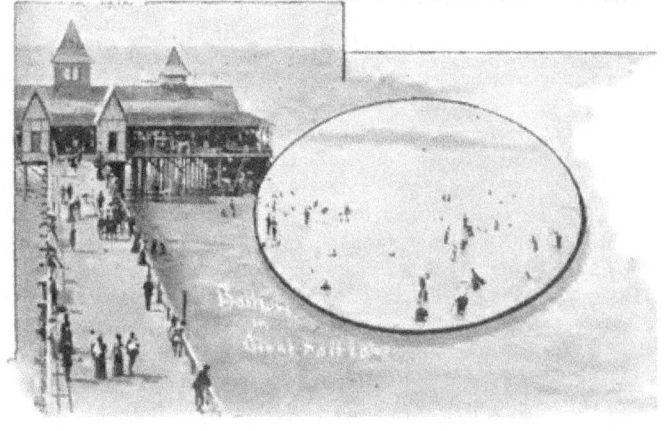

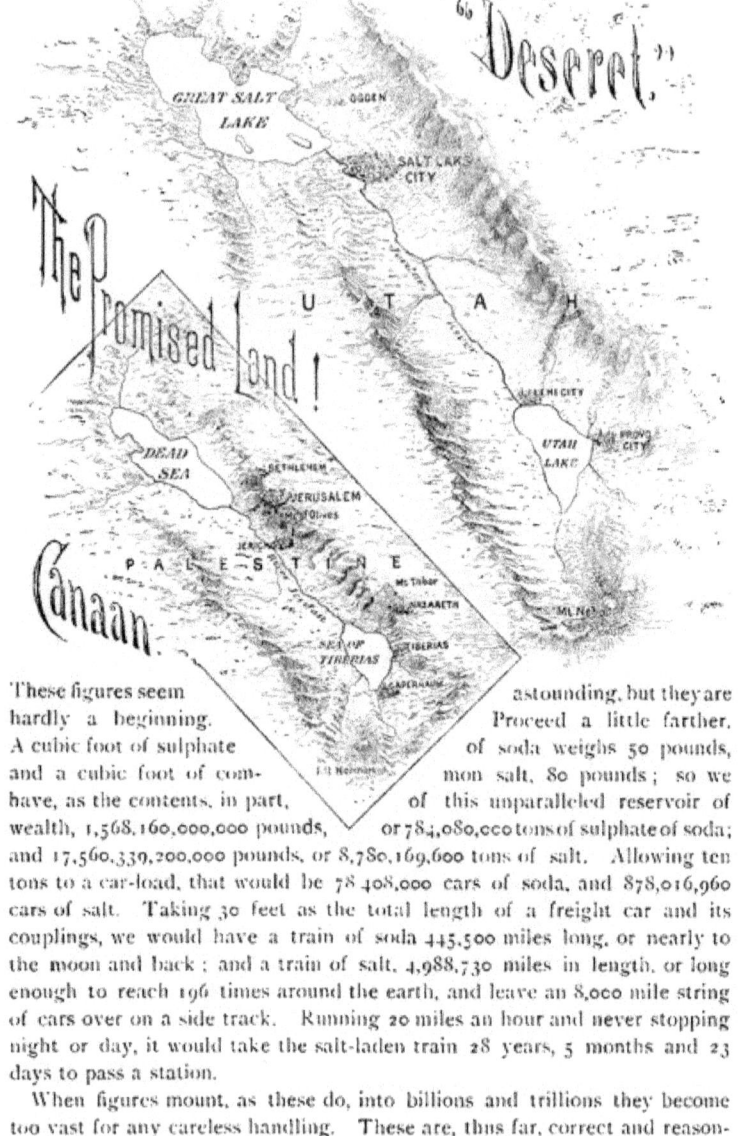

These figures seem astounding, but they are hardly a beginning. Proceed a little farther. A cubic foot of sulphate of soda weighs 50 pounds, and a cubic foot of common salt, 80 pounds; so we have, as the contents, in part, of this unparalleled reservoir of wealth, 1,568,160,000,000 pounds, or 784,080,000 tons of sulphate of soda; and 17,560,339,200,000 pounds, or 8,780,169,600 tons of salt. Allowing ten tons to a car-load, that would be 78,408,000 cars of soda, and 878,016,960 cars of salt. Taking 30 feet as the total length of a freight car and its couplings, we would have a train of soda 445,500 miles long, or nearly to the moon and back; and a train of salt, 4,988,730 miles in length, or long enough to reach 196 times around the earth, and leave an 8,000 mile string of cars over on a side track. Running 20 miles an hour and never stopping night or day, it would take the salt-laden train 28 years, 5 months and 23 days to pass a station.

When figures mount, as these do, into billions and trillions they become too vast for any careless handling. These are, thus far, correct and reasonable, though almost incomprehensible. Carry the computation one step more. The ordinary valuation of sulphate of soda is one cent a pound, or $20 a ton; so our 784,080,000 tons of it would be worth, in the markets of the world, $15,681,600,000. Common salt at a low estimate, is worth a half cent. a pound, or $10 a ton ; our 8,780,169,600 tons of it would consequently have a money value of $87,801,696,000. That is a gigantic, almost inconceivable total for salt and soda, of $103,483,296,000 ; or enough, in two ingredients of this watery wonder of the new world, to pay all the national debts in Christendom, and leave a pretty fair fortune for every man, woman, child and other person in the hemispheric republic of Yankeedoodledoo.

The entire assessed valuation of the United States, including real estate and personal property, under the census of 1880, was $16,902,993,543 ; so the salt and soda of this one mountain-girt lake are worth more than six times as much as the whole forty-nine states and territories of the Union, as shown by the national assessment books ten years ago. Do these figures seem astounding ? The facts are astounding, and the figures but do them justice. The conclusions are inexorable, and the figures, though overwhelming, are absolutely accurate and trustworthy. But cut all the figures in two, halve all the estimates, and we would still have a sum so prodigious, that all the arithmetic classes of creation would stagger before it.

Salt Lake is as entrancing in its beauty, as it is amazing in its material riches. On all our glorious earth, of which Paradise was once a part, no more picturesque and beautiful body of water flashes back from its mirror-like bosom the dazzling radiance of the sunlight. No lovelier lake ripples its melodious love song to the gently wooing breeze ; and no grander inland sea thunders its billowy fury to the shores. The snow-capped Wasatch mountains wall it in on the east and southeast ; the giant Oquirrhs bathe their feet in its southern margin ; the great salt desert, in which Bonneville's exploring expedition came near perishing of thirst and starvation, in 1833. stretches bare and desolate from its western shore, and the wild Promontory Range plunges boldly into its waves for thirty miles on the north. Between the Wasatch mountains and its eastern beach, lies the garden-like valley, while fifteen miles away, on one of its ancient shelving beaches, Salt Lake City, with domes and towers half-hidden in semi-tropical foliage, nestles at the feet of the glacier-crested mountain giants ; and a hundred miles to the southward rises the snowy summit of Nebo to lend a far-off grandeur to the scene.

The tinting of the water reminds one of the iridescent glories of the South Caribbean Sea. Near the shores it is an exquisite opaline green. delicate and wavering. Farther out, this changes into a blue as dazzling as that of the sapphire skies that bend lovingly above it ; and this gradually deepens into royal purple, which darkens and lightens at every touch of the dallying breeze, and every flitting of the golden, fleece-like clouds that fleck the lustrous azure of the heavens. The sunsets are insurpassable in glory in all the grand chariot-course of Phoebus and his flaming steeds. Nature

With awe I watch the sun go down
　　Across the great Salt Lake,
The mountains don their golden crown,
The soaring seagulls circle round,
　　The gentle billows break.

And when I scan what's made for man,
　　To make his heart grow glad,
With wonderment my heart I hush;
I feel the flush of shame's hot blush,
　　Because my soul is sad.

seems to empty all her gorgeous paint-pots on the evening sky, and the day dies, like a vast aerial dolphin, in a conflagration of prismatic splendors.

The whole lake is dotted with magnificently picturesque mountainous islands or islandous mountains, rising out of the blue-green water to a height of from three to five thousand feet. The principal of these wave-washed mountain beauty-spots are Antelope, Stansbury, Fremont, Carrington, Gunnison, Dolphin, Mud, Egg and Hat islands. Antelope Island, the largest of them all, is sixteen miles long and five miles wide, and lies in plain view of Salt Lake City. It towers to an altitude of about four thousand feet above the surface of the lake, and abounds in exquisite scenery. Streams of pure, sweet water tumble down its mountain-sides and canyons; rich grasses flourish everywhere, and it is beautified by groves of trees, thrifty ranches, orchards and gardens. Vast deposits of slate of iridescent hues are found upon it. It has a glorious, gently-sloping beach of snowy sand, and will, beyond all question, some day be the great fashionable bathing-place of interior North America. From present indications it will not be long until every available site for a bathing-ground on the eastern shore of the lake will be appropriated and improved. In 1889, there were 240,000 bathers at the four principal resorts, and over 300,000 in 1890, and among them were tourists from every region of the globe. Antelope Island is an ideal spot for a grand national summer assembly-place; and it seems hardly probable that the enterprising managers of the Rio Grande Western Railway will allow it to lie much longer unimproved. With proper buildings and accommodations, hundreds of thousands of visitors could be annually taken to enjoy the bathing and boating and other aquatic sports and diversions in the most interesting and enchanting region for such purposes on all the continent — if not in all the world.

It may seem preposterous to talk of the finest sea bathing on earth a thousand miles from the ocean; but truth is no less truth because it appears absurd. The sea bathing in Great Salt Lake infinitely surpasses anything of the kind on either the Atlantic or Pacific coasts. The water contains many times more salt and much more soda, sulphur, magnesia, chlorine, bromine and potassium than any ocean water on the globe. It is powerful in medicinal virtues, curing or benefiting many forms of rheumatism, rheumatic gout, dyspepsia, nervous disorders and cutaneous diseases; and it acts like magic on the hair of those unfortunates whose tendencies are to baldheadedness. It is a prompt and potent tonic and invigorant of body and mind, and then there is no end of fun in getting acquainted with its peculiarities. A first bath in it is always as good as a circus, the bather being his or her own amusing trick mule. The specific gravity is but a trifle less than that of the Holy Land Dead Sea, the actual figures with distilled water as unity being, for the ocean 1.027, for Salt Lake 1.107, and for the Dead Sea 1.116. The human body will not and can not sink in it. You can walk out in it where it is fifty feet deep, and your body will stick up out of it like a fishing cork from the shoulders upward. You can sit down in it perfectly secure where it is fathoms deep. Men lie on top of it with their arms crossed under their heads and smoke their cigars. Its buoyancy is indescribable and unimaginable. Any one can float upon it at the first trial ; there is nothing to do but lie down gently upon it — and float. But swimming is an entirely different matter. The moment you begin to "paddle your own canoe" lively and — to the lookers-on — mirth-provoking exercises ensue. When you stick your hands under to make a stroke your feet decline to stay anywhere but on top ; and when, after an exciting tussle with your refractory pedal extremities, you again get them beneath the surface, your hands fly out with the splash and splutter of a half-dozen flutter wheels. If, on account of your brains being heavier than your heels, you chance to turn a somerset and your head goes under, your heels will pop up like a pair of frisky didapper ducks. You can not keep more than one end of yourself under water at once, but you soon learn how to wrestle with its novelties and then it becomes "a thing of beauty" and a joy for any summer day. The water is delightful to the skin, every sensation is exhilarating, and one can not help feeling in it like a gilded cork adrift in a jewel-rimmed bowl of champagne punch. In the sense of luxurious ease with which it envelops the bather it is unrivaled on earth. The only approximation to it is in the phosphorescent waters of the Mosquito Indian coast. The water does not freeze until the thermometric mercury tumbles down to eighteen degrees above zero, or fourteen below the ordinary freezing point. It is as clear as crystal, with a bottom of snow-white sand, and small objects can be distinctly seen at a depth of twenty feet. There is not a fish or any other living thing in all the twenty-five hundred or three thousand square miles of beautiful and mysterious waters, except the yearly increasing swarms of summer bathers. Not a shark or a stingaree to scare the timid swimmer or floater, not a crab or a crawfish to nip the toe of the nervous wader, not a minnow or a frog, a tadpole or a pollywog — nothing that lives, moves, swims, crawls or wiggles. It is the ideal sea-bathing place of the world.

XII

SALT LAKE CITY.

The Inter-Mountain Metropolis — A City of Great Beauty and Infinite Possibilities.

FIFTEEN miles from the southeastern shore of this inland Sea of Wonders, embowered in shade and shrubbery, and recalling glorious pictures of the Orient, is Salt Lake City, the capital and metropolis of Utah, the sacred Zion of the Latter Day Saints, the royal city of the Mormon kingdom and hierarchy. In situation and surroundings it is incomparably the most picturesque and beautiful city in the United States. It sits enthroned, like a queen of the mountains and valleys, upon an ancient beach of the great lake, about a hundred feet above the present level of its waters, and 4,350 feet above the sea. On the east the giant Wasatch mountains, with their crowns of everlasting snow, towering from six to eight thousand feet above it, form a background unsurpassed in grandeur. To the west and northwest, gleaming and glistening like a mighty mirror in the sunshine, which is undimmed three hundred and fifteen days of every year, lies the American Dead Sea, with the Oquirrh mountains dabbling their golden feet in its southern brim. Northward and southward as far as the eye can reach stretches the Edenlike valley, in an unbroken vista of fields and meadows, orchards, vineyards, pastures and gardens — a boundless glory of trees, foliage, fruits and flowers; through which the Jordan, like a silver thread, winds its way to lose itself in the unfathomed mystery of a lake that has many inlets but no outlet.

The city was originally settled by the Mormons under Brigham Young, in July, 1847, and it abounds in monuments and mementoes of these strange people. They laid out the original city in squares, six hundred and sixty-six and two-thirds feet in length; each square containing ten acres. The streets are a hundred and thirty-two feet wide, and every street is shaded by grand old long-armed trees, many of them fruit and flower-bearing. Along both sides of every street flow streams of sparkling mountain water.

Every house in the city is surrounded by green lawns, gardens and orchards, so that one looks in vain for a poor man's home. The humblest, adobe cottage, half hidden in trees, fruit and flowers, becomes a thing of beauty. In fact, the emblem of Mormonism was a Bee Hive, and every man, woman and child had to work at something. Everybody was a producer. No drones were tolerated, and there were no loafers, tramps or beggars. The whole city was abloom with industry and thrift.

Only within the last three or four years has the spirit of modern Gentile progress struck this quaintest, most beautiful and most interesting of North American cities. Its population rose from 20,678 in 1880, to 46,259 in 1890, and it is now between 50,000 and 55,000. The assessed value of property sprang from $16,611,752 in 1889 to $54,353,740 in 1890 ; an increase of 227 per cent. in a single year. As the assessment is on a basis of one-fifth to one-fourth of actual valuation, the true value of real estate and personal property in the city is over $200,000,000; but put it at only double the assessor's figures, and it amounts to $108,707,480, which, in a place of 50,000 population, is an average of more than $2,000 for every inhabitant, within its municipal limits. This has no parallel in any other American city, if it has in the world. Seven new banks were founded during 1890, making sixteen in the city, with an aggregate capital and surplus of $4,853,000, and deposits amounting to $8,225,000 ; an increase, in a year, of over 300 per cent. in capital, and nearly 100 per cent. in deposits. Out of sixty-four cities in the United States having clearing-houses, Salt Lake City outranks thirty-one, including Washington City, the National Capital, with its 200,000 population, and the whole Government and Treasury Department thrown in to boot. The amount invested in new buildings and additions to old ones, in 1890, was $6,226,000 ; in public works $549,000 ; and in street railways $540,000 ; making a grand total of $7,315,000 in these three items of improvement. The city has sixty-five miles of electric street railways ; a hundred miles of admirable streets and drives ; twenty miles of twenty-foot sidewalks ; superb gas and electric lighting systems ; an inexhaustible supply of pure mountain-stream water ; over two hundred prospering manufactories ; twenty-three public and fifteen private schools, and as handsome schoolhouses as any in the country ; the Territorial University, deaf and dumb institute, normal institute and woman's home ; thirty-five churches of all denominations, Catholic, Protestant, Hebrew and Mormon, including the great Temple and Tabernacle ; three excellent hospitals ; thirty benevolent societies ; four live daily papers, and twelve or fifteen weeklies, semi-monthlies and monthlies, including one German and

one Scandinavian publication; six public libraries; two of the finest theatres in the west; a hundred and fifty acres in parks; some of the largest mercantile houses between the Mississippi River and the Pacific Ocean ; six railroads, with over sixty passenger trains daily ; health and pleasure resorts unsurpassed on earth ; a climate as nearly perfect as any place in the temperate zone ; as charming and cultivated society as can be found anywhere ; more beautiful homes and fewer shabby ones than any other city of its size in the Union, and more curious and interesting things than any other place of five times its size in North America.

It is the best amusement-patronizing city of its population in the world. Mapleson, Abbey, Daly, Frohman, Palmer, Theodore Thomas, and all first-class stars and companies crossing the continent, gather large and magnificent audiences in Salt Lake City.

The theatre, built under the auspices of Brigham Young, seats eighteen hundred people, and the new opera-house fourteen hundred, and both are equipped with all modern improvements and conveniences. When these are inadequate to accommodate the crowds, the Mormon authorities are always obliging and polite in allowing their vast Tabernacle to be used ; so it has echoed the divine cadenzas of nearly every famous cantatrice and impressario of recent years.

There are more first-class hotels in Salt Lake City than in St. Louis or Cincinnati. The Knutsford, with three hundred rooms, vies in elegance with the best in the country ; and the million-dollar Ontario, named for the great Utah bonanza mine, will, when completed, rank with the most famous hostelries of the world. The Walker House, The Cullen, The Templeton, The Cliff, and The Union Pacific are all handsome and admirably kept ; and there are a dozen other houses of about the grade of The Laclede in St. Louis, The Sherman in Chicago, and The Gibson in Cincinnati. The Walker House abounds in historic memories and associations. Its hospitable roof has sheltered thousands of noted people, including Dom Pedro, Kalakaua, Grant, Sherman, Patti, Garfield, Edmunds and Harrison ; and dukes, earls, counts, barons and other imported titular celebrities without number.

Many of the churches are handsome and stately edifices ; the school buildings and hospitals would be creditable in any city of a quarter of a million people. There is no city of its size in the United States where the homes are so universally tasteful ; and shade-trees, lawns, fountains, fruit and flowers are so abundant everywhere, that a bird's-eye view from Prospect Hill, or any of the lofty mountain-benches, gives a picture of a vast semi-tropical garden. It is strangely Oriental, and vividly suggestive of Mahomet's reason for refusing to enter Damascus the Beautiful — " It is given unto man but once to enter Paradise, and I will not go into mine on earth."

The Temple Block stands first among the things that must be seen. It is a ten-acre square, surrounded by a massive wall fifteen feet high and five

feet thick. In it stands the magnificent Mormon Temple, the Tabernacle and the Assembly Hall. The Temple is, with the single exception of St Patrick's Cathedral in New York, the grandest and costliest ecclesiastical structure in the country. It was begun in 1853, has cost nearly $6,000,000, and is still unfinished. It is two hundred feet long, a hundred feet wide, and a hundred feet high, with four towers, one at each corner, two hundred and twenty feet in height. The walls are ten feet thick, and the massiveness and solidity of its construction insure its defiance of the ravages of time for ages to come. It is built wholly of snow-white granite from the Cottonwood Canyon ; and, standing on one of the loftiest points in the city, it can be seen for fifty miles up and down the valley.

The Tabernacle, which is just west of the Temple in the same square, is one of the architectural curios of the world. It looks like a vast terrapin-back, or half of a prodigious egg-shell cut in two lengthwise, and is built wholly of iron, glass and stone. It is two hundred and fifty feet long, a hundred and fifty feet wide, and a hundred feet high in the center of the roof, which is a single mighty arch, unsupported by pillar or post, and is said to have but one counterpart on the globe. The walls are twelve feet thick, and there are twenty huge double doors for entrance and exit. The Tabernacle seats 13,462 people, and its acoustic properties are so marvelously perfect that a whisper or the dropping of a pin can be heard all over it. The organ is one of the largest and grandest-toned in existence, and was built here of native woods, by Mormon workmen and artists, at a cost of $100,000. It is fifty-eight feet high, has fifty-seven stops, and contains two thousand six hundred and forty-eight pipes, some of them nearly as large as the chimneys of a Mississippi River steamboat. The choir consists of from two hundred to five hundred trained voices, and the music is glorious beyond description. Much of it is in minor keys, and a strain of plaintiveness mingles with all its majesty and power. All the seats are free, and tourists from all parts of the world are to be found among the vast multitude that assembles at every service Think of seeing the holy communion — broken bread, and water from the Jordan River instead of wine — administered to from six to eight thousand communicants at one time! And fancy the old-time Mormon apostles, bishops, elders and warriors, marching in with from five to twenty wives, and from twenty-five to seventy-five children apiece!

Assembly Hall is of white granite, of Gothic architecture, and has seats for twenty-five hundred. The ceiling is elaborately frescoed with scenes from Mormon history, including the delivery of the golden plates, containing the New Revelation, to the Prophet Joseph Smith, by the Angel Moroni. The Hall contains a superb organ of native woods, and home workmanship.

Just east of Temple Block is another walled square, containing the Mormon Tithing-House and printing-office, and Brigham Young's extensive residence, including the famous Lion House and Bee-Hive House, where eighteen of his wives lived. Across the street to the east is the school-house of his seventy-eight children, which would be a very pretty chapel in an eastern town. Across the street, south of the Lion and Bee-Hive houses, is the superb Amelia Palace, which he built for his nineteenth wife, Amelia Folsom, who was a cousin of Mrs. Grover Cleveland. A block above, on the brow of the hill, is Brigham's grave, and his private graveyard, where all his wives, with perhaps one exception, will ultimately be buried around him, in the order of their marriages, or "sealings" to him; the first one nearest to him, and so on, to the latest and farthest.

The great Zion Coöperative Mercantile Institution, or Mormon store, is one of the sights of the city. It has several acres of floor-room; carries on extensive and various manufacturing operations; and sells and handles everything from a steam-engine and a forty horse-power threshing-machine to a lady's watch and a Parisian trousseau; from a patent hay-rake or a hogshead of sugar, to a baby-wagon, a box of bon-bons, or the latest agony in millinery, scarfs and dress patterns. Its business runs from $4,000,000 to $6,000,000 a year.

Salt Lake City has the model post-office of the United States. When President Harrison and his party visited the city in the early part of 1891, Postmaster-General Wanamaker was so pleased with the perfection of all its arrangements that he requested photographs of every department of it sent to Washington, to be used as patterns for other offices. Postmaster Benton, to whom the credit of its admirable features belongs, was formerly a trusted agent of the Rio Grande Western Railway, and consequently received his training in a first-class school of efficiency.

The Chamber of Commerce Building is a handsome four-story structure of stone and brick, and contains an extensive and valuable library, and a wonderful collection of Utah products — agricultural, mineral, pastoral and textile. Offices of the Traffic, Accounting and Financial Departments of the Rio Grande Western Railway occupy two floors of the block.

The Deseret Museum is well worth a visit, having a vast number of curious and interesting things on exhibition — Utah beasts, birds, reptiles, insects, minerals, gems, fruits, flowers, freaks and queeriosities. Fort Douglas, a full regimental post, on a high mountain bench or plateau just east of the city, is one of the most picturesque in all the dominions of Uncle Samuel. It commands as glorious a view as lies out of doors.

Salt Lake City is surrounded by lovely pleasure-grounds and unsurpassable health-resorts. The mountains and canyons afford an endlessly varied field for summer-tourist recreation; and medicated waters, potent in healing virtues, gush forth in a hundred places. The most famous of these are the Warm Springs, within the city limits, and the Hot Springs, about four miles out — both on electric street-car lines. The water of Hot Springs has a temperature of 128°, and the flow is over 20,000 gallons an hour. It

possesses all the efficacy of the Arkansas Hot Springs water, and is a sovereign remedy in all ordinary cases of rheumatism, rheumatic gout, scrofulous diseases, mineral poisoning, ulcers, abscesses and cutaneous eruptions of nearly every sort. Thousands of cures have been wrought here; some of them seemingly almost miraculous. The water of the Warm Springs, with a temperature of 103°, is piped into a superb natatorium in the heart of the city; and it is but a question of time — and a short time at that — when the waters of the Hot Springs and of the Great Salt Lake will be rendered equally convenient to the city bather. The invalid here has the advantage of a climate that is as nearly perfect as can be found; dry, bracing, combining the salt air of the sea with the pure and rarified air of the mountains; where the sun shines nearly every day in the year; where there is no fog, miasma, or malaria, and where the blizzards and sand-storms that afflict other health-resort regions are unknown.

Salt Lake City has profitable openings for nearly every variety of industrial enterprises, and for a constantly increasing number of wholesale and retail mercantile houses. Situated almost exactly midway between Denver and San Francisco, the city has tributary to it a grand and growing empire, rich in all materials of commerce. With its long arms of railway rapidly reaching out north, south, east and west, into Idaho, Nevada, Arizona, New Mexico, and Southern Colorado, it is destined to become the undisputed Metropolis of the vast Inter-Mountain Realm.

www.ingramcontent.com/pod-product-compliance
Lightning Source LLC
Chambersburg PA
CBHW032241080426
42735CB00008B/958